Grief Healing Techniques

Grief Healing Techniques

Step-by-Step Support for Working Through Grief and Loss

CALISTOGA PRESS

Contents

Introduction

Have you suffered the loss of a loved one—a spouse, a partner, a parent, a child, or someone else who had been a vital part of your life and about whom you cared deeply? Have you come face-to-face with some other personal loss: a divorce, a health crisis, an abrupt dismissal from a job or failure of a business, the death of a cherished pet, or saying good-bye to a home? Has your loss left you sad, confused, angry, and full of questions that seem to have no answers?

If any of these examples describe your current situation, chances are that you are experiencing grief, a natural, normal response to encountering any major loss. Grief is an emotional distress that you suffer when someone or something close to you has been taken away. It is a multidimensional experience that can affect you physically, emotionally, socially, and even spiritually. Grief can come upon women or men at any age or stage of life, and it cuts across all socioeconomic levels. No one escapes loss; whatever your philosophical or spiritual belief system, experiencing a significant loss and the subsequent grieving can shake up your psyche. When grief strikes, it can feel as if the world has been pulled out from under you. The sudden onset of deep sorrow can occur whether you had time to prepare for a loss or whether it roared in without warning. You might wonder if the dark storm clouds will ever disappear. You may even find yourself replaying the same thoughts over and over in your mind:

I can't believe this has happened!
What am I going to do now?
I just want to be alone.

No one understands what I'm going through.
Why do I feel so numb?
I don't want to eat anything.
I just want to sleep.
Am I ever going to feel any better?

The painful feelings and disturbing moods that can take over your life while you are grieving may be unlike anything you have ever experienced. Even if some of these feelings are familiar, you may be caught off guard by how intense they are or how they linger. This, too, is natural. Grief is simply a part of our human condition, a natural by-product of loving and caring deeply. In fact, as difficult as it may be for you to believe today, grief is both a natural and a *healthy* process for coping with a major loss, such as the death of a loved one. When you better understand grief, and learn and practice some of the helpful tools and resources that have guided many people like you safely through the storm, you too can come through.

You may never "get over it," but you can find constructive ways to move on as you begin to heal physically and emotionally. Food will taste better. Sleep will once again fit your regular rhythm of life. People you may have been avoiding will no longer appear as unwanted intrusions but rather as vital sources of support, or rich opportunities for connection. Over time, you can reclaim your life and renew your spirit. You can learn to laugh, and even to love again. You may tap a new strength or a degree of resilience that you never thought you had.

This book is designed to help you navigate through the grief journey successfully. It will help you to understand and cope with the process of grieving. People who suffer a major loss often feel as if they are in the midst of a crash course on grief, because few learn how grief works until it grips them unexpectedly. This guide will help you grasp and understand just what you need to know right now. In the following chapters, you will gain a greater awareness of the many painful side effects associated with grief and the reasons for them. You will find helpful and productive ways to weather the storm and allow the sun to come out again in *your* life.

One of the most important realities to understand about the grief process is that there is no magic formula to managing grief, no one-size-fits-all system that will work for everyone who has suffered loss. Each person grieves in their own way. Your grief journey may not look the same as others you may know, even if they have experienced a loss similar to yours. Yes, there may be commonality, some similar reference points along the trail, but there are likely to be many differences as well. If you discover a healthy resource or practice that assists you, stick with it, even if others do not find it particularly useful or even think it a bit unusual. Similarly, if someone suggests an approach that they are convinced will help and it just does not click for you, be willing to reject that idea, or at least set it aside for the time being. As you make the commitment to fully enter your grief process and begin to practice some of the exercises and strategies in this book, you will learn which avenues for healing and growth will be the most effective for you, thus cultivating your own grief path.

Grief follows no definite timetable. You may hear claims that grief should last a certain number of weeks or months, or that you should be fully back into your regular life by some specific point after your loss. Though likely well intentioned, such rigid expectations are misguided and sometimes come with harsh judgments. "You should be over it by now," friends or family members may tell you. The reality is that grief does not move in a straight line. It may more closely resemble a roller coaster, with peaks and valleys and frequent, abrupt changes of speed and intensity. The goal is to open your eyes and know where you are going, and gradually to learn to be able to control the ride.

As you begin to read this book, it does not matter how long it has been since you suffered your loss. You may be reaching out for guidance within days or weeks of the death of a loved one, or whatever your painful loss may be. Alternately, it may have been several months or even a year or longer since the storm hit, but the damage is only now showing up in your life. What matters is that you have recognized the need to understand and manage your grief, so that you can land back on your feet again and gradually move forward in a life that will never be the same, but can still be rewarding and fulfilling.

So let's begin.

CHAPTER 1

Understanding Grief

"You seem so different," your friends and family may tell you. They know that you have suffered a painful loss, and they are truly concerned for your well-being. With good intentions, they may offer evidence of how you are not acting like yourself:

- You seem sad most of the time and may reject invitations to go out to a movie or join in some other activity to help lift you out of your gloom.

- You may act jittery and easily lash out in anger when someone says or does something that rubs you the wrong way, even when they assure you that they are "just trying to help."

- You aren't eating enough to stay healthy, even when others bring your favorite foods and suggest that you "try just a little."

- You look pale and haggard, and your expression hardly seems to change.

- You stay in bed late, and then may resist getting dressed or beginning daily tasks for hours longer.

- You carefully avoid any physical reminders of whom or what you have lost.

- When encouraged to talk about your feelings, you refuse or even become angry.

One of the difficult aspects of facing a major loss can be feeling as if the people who care about you do not understand what you are going through. Moreover, it is possible that even those who are close to you may not always recognize or accept the simple reality: *You are grieving.*

It is even more difficult for others to acknowledge the effects of grief and to respect your need to grieve if you are not able to acknowledge it yourself. That, unfortunately, is an all too frequent by-product of grieving. You may know that you are behaving differently, but it may take time to fully grasp what's really happening. You might just assume there is something wrong with you, without having a clear idea of the underlying cause. How you appear to others is only a small part of the picture. Signs of grief may be present in thoughts and feelings that you may be keeping to yourself:

- You keep replaying in your mind the final moments, hours, or days before the loss happened, searching for something, *anything*, that could have been done to change the outcome.

- You feel waves of anger or even rage toward those you believe are responsible for the loss, whether it is the drunk driver who caused the accident, the doctors who couldn't make your loved one better, the company that let you go, or anyone or anything else that "made" it happen. You may even feel anger toward your loved one for leaving you.

- You feel guilt for whatever you believe you did or did not do to cause the loss to occur, perhaps saying to yourself, "It's all my fault." Or you feel guilty for not expressing your love enough while your beloved was here.

- When someone who means well says, "I know how you feel," or tries to connect with you by telling you about their own struggles, you may push them away or even want to scream at them, "No, you don't know how I feel! No one knows how I feel!"

- You feel a sense of helplessness or even hopelessness about the future. You may think that your life is ruined.

All of these actions, thoughts, and feelings may seem to further contribute to the mounting evidence that you really are different. You may know yourself to be generally kind, caring, understanding, and patient. Rather than trying to chase people away, you usually enjoy their company and may be very socially active. Up to this point, you may have tried to follow healthy patterns of eating and sleeping as well as maintaining a positive outlook on life. So when you're suddenly going around sad, angry, and lethargic most of the time, you may think that there really *must* be something wrong. After all, you're not the only one who has suffered a loss, right? Other people have it worse than you do. They have been hit with more severe trauma or tragedies, or they must deal with more difficult day-to-day life circumstances than you. Why can't you just snap out of it and get on with life?

If you have had any of these thoughts or drawn any of these conclusions about what you are going through, take a deep breath and allow this truth to sink in: *There is nothing wrong with you. You are just grieving, and it is a natural and necessary process. Simply put, it is human nature to grieve after suffering a loss.*

The Physical and Biological Nature of Grief

Let's look at the evidence of how and why all those frustrating and often frightening manifestations of grief are entirely normal. It is helpful to understand that when you suffer a loss and enter a grieving process, whether or not you are aware of doing so, your body goes into a state of stress. The stress of loss is both mental and physical, disrupting your brain and your biological rhythms. Physiological changes result that can affect your nervous system, your immune system, and even your cardiovascular system. Your whole body can just feel out of sorts.

Physical symptoms of grief may manifest in many different ways. Here are ten of the more frequent experiences for those in the aftermath of a major loss:

1. **Loss of appetite.** In the first several days or even weeks after enduring a loss, you may find it almost impossible to eat. Regular

meals are out of the question, and it may take a great effort on your part even to nibble on the small snacks that others urge you to accept. Your body just isn't interested in food.

2. **Stomachaches and nausea.** When your nerves are shot from the shock and stress of your loss, it is natural to experience a degree of gastrointestinal distress, even if that symptom was not previously a common one for you.

3. **Severe headaches.** That pounding in your head is a physical sensation, and it is often accentuated by an emotional response. It is as if some force keeps banging home the reality that your life will never be the same again.

4. **Extreme fatigue.** Undergoing severe stress can feel as if your body is weighed down by a ton of bricks. No wonder you do not want to leave the house or even get out of bed.

5. **Accelerated heart rate or shakiness.** Uncertainty about what's going to happen to you in the aftermath of your loss can trigger an increase in adrenaline and a sense of panic resulting in temporarily increased heart rate and/or minor tremors.

6. **Difficulty sleeping.** When your body is in a state of grief-induced shock, it is hard to settle down into a restful, peaceful state. Sleep may come in fits and starts, often punctuated with endless mind chatter about what happened to you and how the change is making you feel about life.

7. **Sudden angry outbursts.** Frustrated outbursts that have no immediate trigger can be interpreted as your body's way of expressing its stress overload. Yelling "I can't take this anymore!" or "It's not fair!" may be in part your body's attempt to alleviate grief-related stress.

8. **Prolonged crying or sobbing that can briefly trigger a sense of choking.** Like other physical symptoms, this sensation can be scary when it occurs. You feel a loss of control and may worry that you are about to suffer something even worse. Try to relax and

breathe deeply, reminding yourself that this is another manifestation of grief and your body's attempt to compensate. Within a short time, the sensation will likely pass.

9. **Temporary confusion or absentmindedness.** If you easily forget the day of the week, or where you left your glasses, or what you had agreed to do an hour ago, this is simply another symptom of the stress caused by your loss. Wandering around your house aimlessly is not a sign that you are "going crazy."

10. **Inability to concentrate.** You may be watching a movie with your family and suddenly realize that you do not know what happened ten minutes ago, even though you thought you were paying attention.

If you are experiencing a few or several of these physical symptoms, it is helpful to understand that they are often signs of your body's attempt to absorb your grief. You may find that these symptoms will come and go over time, or lessen in their intensity. If you accept what is happening as normal, you can fret about them a little less, which in turn can help to reduce your stress.

Other signs of grief may also be showing up in your day-to-day life. You may notice that you still feel shocked at what happened, even if the loss occurred weeks or even months ago. When you are able to fall asleep, you may be awakened by disturbing dreams of your beloved or whatever you have lost, and you may have waking moments of imagining that your loved one is still here. You may be losing weight, which is not at all surprising if you are having trouble eating. If you are grieving over the loss of a loved one, you may find yourself engulfed by fears of your own mortality. Again, all of these experiences fall into the category of natural and normal responses to grief. Do not be overly concerned that there is something wrong with you. With time, healthy choices, and focused attention on your grief journey, most of the symptoms will likely lessen in frequency and intensity, or eventually dissipate.

You may notice that your loss is having a ripple effect on your life. On top of the actual loss you have suffered, you may be experiencing the loss of a sense of security, the loss of a familiar lifestyle, the loss of status, the loss of a sense of belonging somewhere or with some group, or the loss of a dream. This, too, is part of grief. Major loss usually involves much more than what first meets the eye. The grief triggered by loss can affect everything that you do, and it can show up in every area of your life.

Loss can sometimes come in bunches: the death of a loved one followed by the loss of a job. Multiple losses can send you into compound grief, adding to your despair and anxiety. It is normal and natural that even though you have grieved over one loss, a new loss will still hit you hard.

As you thoughtfully begin to redefine all those "different" behaviors and feelings as a normal and necessary part of grieving, you may discover that you are able to relax just a bit more about what you are experiencing. Part of the healing process is understanding and accepting the reality that your physical and mental state has been disrupted or knocked out of whack, and that it is going to take time and care to return to a more harmonious existence.

Ten Myths and Misconceptions about Grief

A necessary step in successfully managing your grief is to set aside what you may have always believed or what you may have been told by others and confront the myths and misconceptions about grief. Here are ten common myths:

1. **Grief should last for a few months or a year at most.** There is no right or wrong time frame for the healthy process of grieving to unfold. For many people, the grief process lasts much longer than a year. It will take as long as it needs to take . . . for *you*. Pressuring yourself to hurry up and get past the grief will actually disrupt the natural healing rhythm of grief and prolong your pain. Instead of counting the weeks or months that you have been grieving, focus your attention and awareness on how well you are practicing the healthy and productive steps related to your grief journey.

2. **Grief proceeds through clearly defined stages.** You will learn about some of the most common phases or responses to grief after loss in the next chapter, but it is important to understand that these are merely possible reference points on your grief journey. It is entirely possible that some or all of the many phases or forms of grief will not resonate with you. That does not mean you have veered off the trail toward health and healing. It simply means that you are finding your own way.

3. **Choosing to pursue counseling for grief is a sign of weakness.** Some people find the needed support and guidance to manage the grief process without counseling, but for many others, counseling becomes an essential and invaluable tool in dealing with a loss. Many of those who benefit from grief counseling had been leading emotionally healthy lives without the need for counseling or therapy before suffering a loss. They found that, rather than a sign of weakness, choosing counseling for this experience was a sign of wisdom and strength. Counseling helped provide shape and direction to their grief journey and opened the door to a new set of helpful resources and strategies.

4. **You need to avoid emotional vulnerability to stay strong for your family.** Denying or avoiding your natural emotions slows or even sabotages your healing. Your family cares about you and wants to see you regain your health and strength. Your willing-ness to enter fully into the feelings and experiences of grief, along with your ability to explain to your family what you are learning about the realities of the grief journey, will help reassure them that you are on the right track.

5. **It is improper to laugh or to feel a profound sense of relief while grieving.** It is very natural from time to time to find yourself laughing about the loved one you have lost or the life situation that has been taken away from you. Telling funny stories about the shared past with that person or laughing almost uncontrollably at a private joke you held with them are healthy ways to honor their memory and the love you still feel for them. Crying is not the only form of expressing those feelings. It is also

normal to feel a sense of relief that the loss has come, especially if it was preceded by a long period of pain and suffering. The relief does not mean that you "wanted" the loss to come, only that the death or other final point of a life situation at least put an end to one phase of suffering.

6. **Grief should be easier if the loss was a long time in coming.** Many people are caught by surprise because they assume that if they lose a loved one who is elderly or who had been in the dying stages for months or even years, they are "prepared" for the loss and it won't hurt so much when it comes. The reality is that we grieve the loss itself and the connection we have felt with that person or life situation, regardless of age or manner of passing. While losing a loved one through a sudden accident or illness can certainly be more traumatic, especially in the immediate aftermath, the sting of a loss is still felt no matter what the circumstances.

7. **It won't hurt as much if we remember what was wrong with our relationship with that person or life situation.** Many of us have had conflict in our relationship with a parent or another family member, and the difficult feelings about that relationship will not necessarily disappear when that person is gone. However, that doesn't mean the loss won't hurt as much as it would if the relationship had been "perfect." The love that you felt toward that person (or pet, or job), and the connection you had established, will almost inevitably pour through during the grief process. Expecting that it will be lessened because of previous conflicts is usually misguided.

8. **It is wrong to suddenly have strong feelings about a loss from a long time ago.** This is another natural response during the grief process. As you allow yourself to open up to the deep sadness from your current loss, previous grief related to a loss from long ago may be stirred up. If this happens, welcome it. It may be an opportunity to address unresolved grief from the past, or simply a time to honor the love and connection of someone or something else you have lost. It does not mean that you love or care any less for whatever you have just lost. You will likely find your attention shifting back to that void soon enough.

9. **It is better to just ignore or stifle the pain.** Trying to repress your pain is like trying to shut off the water faucet when you have a burst water pipe. It simply will not work. More than that, you are trying to dam up the natural healing process of grief. It is far healthier to allow the pain to be pain, and to find ways of supporting your body and mind through the natural process of grieving.

10. **Life will eventually look and feel "normal" again.** Loss is permanent. That loved one is not returning. The surgery that removed a part of your body is irreversible. The job or career or other life situation that was lost is still gone. If you are looking for a state of normalcy that is equal to everything returning to the way it used to be, you are setting yourself up for ongoing frustration and disappointment. Change after loss is inevitable. The pain of the loss may never completely go away, although you can certainly expect it to lessen its hold on you. You do have the capacity to rebuild your life, and the potential for joy and happiness will grow over time. But the "old normal" may never return as you come to terms with the "new normal."

If you found yourself believing some or many of these common myths and misconceptions about grief, do not feel bad. These ideas are commonly accepted, and friends and family who mean well may also believe that they are true. You know better now, and even if it takes a while to let go of the myth, recognize that this too is natural. Learning about grief, and putting into practice what you learn, takes time.

If you had already recognized the reality behind most or even all of these myths, that is a good sign. Nevertheless, you will find it helpful to reinforce those truths as you take new steps forward on your grief journey.

Now let's proceed together to the next step.

CHAPTER 2

Embracing Your Feelings

At this stage of your grief journey, you may have begun to accept the concept that grief is a normal and necessary part of healing after loss. Perhaps you have also come to understand that expressing your feelings is a natural and critical component of grieving. But what if, most of the time, you find yourself not feeling any particular emotion—no sadness, no anxiety, no anger? Mostly you just experience yourself as being numb. What do you do?

First, keep in mind that it does not help to judge your grief experience. Being numb much of the time is just what is happening right now. It is not wrong. You have not sabotaged all possibilities for healing and rediscovering the goodness in life. Having this attitude of acceptance will allow you room to make new choices without blaming yourself for "not doing it right."

Next, understand that numbness can have its place in the grief journey. In fact, it is normal to go numb in the early days after suffering a loss. Numbness can protect you from being engulfed or overwhelmed with extreme sadness or fear. Soon after the death of a loved one, for example, it is not at all unusual to "zone out" during the funeral or memorial service. The feelings at that moment may simply be too much to take on, whereas they may crop up often in the next few days or weeks.

You may have a similar experience if your loss involves a medical crisis—when the doctor gives you the bad news, or the surgery is incomplete—and you just feel numb. Or, if your loss takes the form of being fired or losing your business, you may go numb after being handed the layoff notice or when the doors are closed for good.

If this happens to you, do not be upset if someone misinterprets your behavior. "How could you just sit there through the whole funeral with that vacant expression?" a family member or friend may demand, with the implication being that somehow you do not care enough about the beloved or that you were being disrespectful. Remember that you were simply taking care of yourself. Your numbness formed a protective shield.

You may notice that you go numb after you have just begun to feel an intense emotion. The tears start to flow, and they just keep pouring out for several minutes. You may get panicky, fearful that they won't stop and you will not be able to regain control of yourself and your actions. You stuff the feeling back inside. Going numb is a "flight" response to escape the torrent of tears.

This, too, can be a normal part of the grief process, for a while. The problem emerges if numbness prevails as your most frequent state of being and your feelings remain mostly submerged for weeks, months, or even years. That problem can become magnified if you encourage the numbness response by turning to a crutch, such as drinking alcohol in excess or watching mindless TV programs for hours, day after day. Behaviors like these push you further and further away from the feelings that are waiting to be expressed.

Conversely, when you make the choice to stay open to your feelings and find safe ways to fully experience them—as often as you need to and for as long as necessary each time—you are taking a positive step in your grief journey. Just as continually going around in a state of numbness can block your healing, so too can pretending that you must be "okay" because you are not having strong emotions. You might say to yourself and to those who care about you, "I'm not crying all the time. I'm not screaming in anger or agony. I don't have a problem with grief. I don't need help." In reality, you may simply be avoiding the natural expression of those feelings, an expression that will help you gradually to feel better instead of remaining seemingly okay.

You may find yourself afraid of feeling your emotions, because you are just not used to doing so. You have always been in control, keeping your head on straight so you can do your job and function effectively in your life. Choosing to express your feelings can be a big change.

Making room for your feelings may require tuning out some of the standards or beliefs that come from the outside. You may need to reject the outmoded, stereotypical notions that "only weak men cry," or that "big girls don't cry." In reality, crying, and every other emotional expression, are natural responses to painful loss for any human being. It is actually a sign of strength.

You may need to overcome other misguided beliefs and habits held by your family, such as pretending that emotions are not real or are to be avoided in the name of staying sane or rational. It may be necessary to reevaluate influences of your culture or environment that could discourage you from allowing your feelings to have their place.

Once you adopt a more accepting attitude toward your feelings, they will naturally begin to show up more regularly. Still, you may find yourself afraid that the feelings triggered by your grief will just be too much to handle and will take you too far from your comfort zone. If you are prepared for the emotions that you are most likely to encounter, you will likely find them easier to deal with when they arrive. Here are five of the more common emotional states during grief:

1. **Shock or disbelief.** This response is not surprising or alarming if it occurs immediately after suffering the loss, especially if you lose a loved one through sudden death. "I just can't believe this is real," you might say. However, it is also natural for those feelings of shock and disbelief to continue to pop up from time to time. The dramatic change resulting from the loss is difficult to absorb fully.

2. **Sadness.** For many of those who are grieving, sadness may be the dominant feeling for quite some time. Loss is painful, often feeling as if someone just drove a dagger into your heart. Whether the sadness is expressed as crying, sobbing, or just an empty, aching sensation, it is likely to visit you often and frequently.

3. **Anger.** You may yell, scream, or throw objects against a wall. "I don't want to live alone!" you shout. Or you declare, "This isn't fair!" Loss may not be fair, but it is real, and so is the anger that comes in response to the loss. Sometimes that anger may even

spill out in absolute rage. While it is important to avoid directing your anger at another person, accepting your feelings of anger will help it to recede gradually.

4. **Fear or anxiety.** It is natural to feel afraid or anxious about how you are going to cope with the profound change that comes from your loss. If loss comes in the form of the death of a loved one, it is also normal to fear that you are going to die soon, too. You may find yourself worried about how long your grief will last and what condition you will be in as it goes on for months and months. As with anger, acceptance will loosen the grip of fear.

5. **Guilt.** As discussed in Chapter 1, it is common for those who are grieving to blame themselves for what happened and search for what they could have done differently. It is also not unusual to feel guilty for being so wrapped up in grief that you are not as present as you would like to be for your family or friends. Another form of grief after a death is to feel guilty for being the one who survived. "Why didn't I die, too, so we could have stayed together?" you may ask. It is important not to become consumed by guilt, but when it surfaces, it is helpful simply to recognize its place in your experience.

You may notice other feelings in your grief journey, or you may simply be feeling intense waves of the same emotion, such as sadness, again and again. That is natural. You may discover that your dominant emotion shifts after a period of time. You may progress from sadness to anger, for example. It is important to remember that emotions are unpredictable and sporadic. They can come upon you at any time, in any situation. A natural trigger for grief, such as opening the door to a deceased child's bedroom, may prompt deep wells of sadness to swirl up. But so can the seemingly most mundane and innocent moments.

Your feelings also do not necessarily fit any definite design. That is true for the grief process itself. Remember, each person grieves differently. There is no right or wrong way. Some theories about grief suggest that the grief journey can be marked by specific phases or stages. You may be familiar with what are often referred to as the five stages of grief, first presented by Elizabeth Kübler-Ross in her ground-breaking book, *On Death and Dying*. Those stages are:

1. Denial

2. Anger

3. Bargaining

4. Depression

5. Acceptance

The terrain of the grief journey has been described as covering a period of shock or denial, then an obsession with the loss, followed by a deeper despair, and then eventually recovery. Other grief specialists have pointed to just two basic stages: one, accepting the reality of the loss itself; and two, accepting the impact of the loss on your life and finding meaning in the experience of grieving and moving forward. Another way to look at the process may be through the following phases:

1. Coming to terms with what happened.

2. Expressing and working through your feelings.

3. Adjusting to your "new normal" and discovering the person you have become through the grief process.

4. Making room for an enduring connection with the person or life situation that you have lost.

As you become more and more comfortable with the idea of embracing your feelings and practicing other tools and strategies on the grief journey, you may find that one or more of these maps of the grief journey resonate with you. In that case, they may be helpful to you in providing a context for your experience as markers to find along the trail. However, your response to grief may not look like *any* of these models. In fact, your grief journey may not seem to be following any organized or logical progression or path at all. Rather, it may take the form of a series of zigzags as you do your best to follow along. If that is happening for you, there is nothing wrong with your experience. You are simply reinforcing the reality that every grief journey is unique. Do not let anyone tell you how you *should* feel, or what state of grief you should be in, or what phase you need to enter next.

In fact, it can be harmful to try to force yourself to conform to some outlined system of dealing with a loss. It is entirely possible, for example, that you may never experience intense anger as part of any phase or period of grief. This does not mean you are failing to make progress, or that you have "skipped" a required step. If you are allowing yourself to have feelings, and your life is moving toward health and healing, do not worry about the absence of a particular emotion in your process. Do not allow any rigid outline of grief stages to become another "should" or a potential source of guilt if you do not follow it. Your feelings, and the grief journey itself, will take you where you need to go.

Making Room to Feel

What do you do if you have the intention to embrace your feelings but find that they are seldom showing up as you go through your day? You do not feel especially numb, and you are not aware of trying to suppress your emotions. But for one reason or another, your feelings just tend to be held at bay. Should you try to *make* them come out?

Again, grief is not about forcing anything. It is about accepting and allowing a natural process to unfold. However, because it is so very important to open up to your feelings, you may find it helpful to both allow and gently *encourage* their expression.

How? Let's say you have a vague sense that you are indeed sad about the loss you have suffered, and you are aware that not allowing room for the sadness may slow your recovery. Here are ways you can allow your sadness a chance to rise to the surface:

- Look over some photos or other tangible reminders of your loved one. It may help to simply speak their name aloud a few times or say, "I miss you, _____."

- Watch a sad, familiar movie. If it made you cry before you suffered your loss, you may cry again now—and the tears this time may open the door to feeling the real sadness over your loss.

- Listen to some of your beloved's favorite songs, or perhaps songs that you enjoyed together. It may help to close your eyes briefly as you recall those moments of joy and union.

- Start a journal in which you record your day-to-day experiences since your loss. Then reflect back and write about those final days and hours before the loss, and venture even further back to some special memories that you shared together.

- Sit for a few moments in quiet meditation or prayer. Sometimes just taking a break from the business of life is enough to let the feelings in.

- Visit an Internet or in-person support group for those in grief, especially if you are likely to come across people there who have suffered a similar or comparable loss to yours. You may feel an urge to join in one of the discussion groups or other public postings, or you may choose to hold back and simply read and witness the sharing of others. It is quite possible that someone else's story will help you get access to your own emotions.

When you do decide to take an active step to make room for your feelings, take care to establish a safe space where you feel comfortable and are not likely to be disturbed. You may need to tell family members that you are visiting that safe place and need privacy for a while.

After you have settled into your safe space, just sit for a few moments, breathe deeply, and gently explore whether a feeling may be arising. Let's say you have a vague notion that feelings of anger may be bubbling under the surface. Try this: Grab a pillow, and as you squeeze or hit it, focus on what might be making you angry. See if there are words that accompany this feeling: "You weren't supposed to ever leave me!" or "It isn't fair!" You might choose instead to take out a piece of paper and use crayons or markers to draw an image of this anger.

As you begin to have positive experiences with letting your feelings come out, consider setting aside a specific time every day, or every other day, to return to your safe space. You might continue to experiment with different approaches to allow or invite your feelings to emerge, or you may choose to just be quietly present and see what feelings arise. This will give you another opportunity to practice acceptance of any experience on your own unique grief journey.

As you become more open to the expression of your feelings, you may be surprised to find that you really do not fall apart. The world does not end. You still feel intact. This will give you confidence to continue to express even more feelings that may have been hidden.

Keep in mind, though, that you do not want to rush your expression of feelings. It is usually best to move slowly, giving yourself opportunities to explore and feel emotions related to your loss while still maintaining a balance in your life. You still need those occasions when your emotions are temporarily at rest. It is perfectly okay if you still find yourself wanting to spend some periods of time "vegging out"—watching mindless TV or even staring at the walls. The difference now is that you know such behavior is temporary and that you have the skills and the tools to find the time and the means to embrace your feelings actively.

Notice that all of these options are steps that you can take by yourself. You may find that you are able to embrace your feelings and make valuable progress in your grief journey on your own. However, it is important to keep in mind that it is not advisable to attempt to manage your entire grief process alone. For most of us, the full experience is simply too much. Additionally, there is so much to be gained from reaching out for the support of other people. These may include family and friends currently in your life, or new contacts on a similar journey who you make by seeking to connect with. The next chapter will discuss why reaching out to others is important and how you can successfully manage those relationships while grieving.

When you consider the pool of people who may be able to offer you support during your grief process, counselors or other healthcare professionals are apt to have a prominent place on the list. In fact, you may find that turning to a professional for guidance and support may be a necessary step at some point in your grief journey. Before proceeding to the next chapter, it will be helpful to take an inventory of your current grief experience and consider whether it may be time to call upon a counselor for help right now.

Ten Signs That It May Be Time to Seek Professional Help with Your Grief

1. **You have frequent bouts of hopelessness.** While occasionally feeling hopeless about the future may be natural, if you find that it is happening more and more often, a counselor can help you explore such feelings in a safe way. If your hopeless feelings are leading you to indulge in alcohol or drug use, or if they are accompanied by suicidal thoughts, it is critical that you obtain help right away.

2. **You spend considerable time searching for your departed loved one.** It is natural to find yourself occasionally calling out for the one you have lost in a moment of temporarily forgetting what has happened. But if you're frequently roaming your house or apartment actively searching for that person, and even expecting to find them there, that's something to share with an experienced counselor.

3. **You lose an excessive amount of weight and become weak.** It is natural to suffer some loss of appetite, but if your lack of eating continues for a prolonged period and results in significant weight loss, you will certainly want to be checked out by your doctor. A counselor can offer further assistance in helping you better manage your feelings and adopt healthier self-care strategies while the grief continues.

4. **Your feelings of guilt become pervasive.** If you find yourself obsessing over how this loss is all your fault to the point of pushing all other emotions aside, a counselor can help you see how you have become stuck and point you toward ways to find a better balance in your feelings and perspective.

5. **You wish you had died instead of your beloved, and you count the days until your death will come.** Feeling lost or left behind when a loved one dies is natural and can trigger wonderment about why you did not die, too. However, if such feelings shift toward an active death wish, professional help is needed.

6. **You notice alarming physical sensations, such as shortness of breath or slowed, slurred speech.** This is another indicator that a medical checkup may be needed to rule out problems that extend beyond normal grief and require immediate attention.

7. **You demonstrate an inability to perform simple daily tasks required for your basic well-being.** This issue is especially important to deal with if you live alone. Even if you live with family members who are willing to help pick up some of the pieces when you cannot function at your usual level, you may need to call upon outside support if you are so distraught and weak that you cannot dress or bathe yourself, or prepare food.

8. **Your loss of appetite suddenly shifts to a pattern of overeating, which may be accompanied by nausea or vomiting.** A counselor can help you sift through the emotional causes of your altered eating habits and prevent the pattern from getting worse.

9. **You cannot trust anyone or anything, and you are constantly fighting with family members or others close to you.** Yes, anger and frustration can often spill out unintentionally toward those who love us, especially if they tell us how we should feel or insist that we should "get over it." You can expect some strain or conflict in your relationships while in the midst of the grief process. However, you do not want the burden of constant conflict or the weight of thinking that *no one* can be trusted. A counselor can help you explore the feelings behind your attitude and suggest strategies for dealing with loved ones while taking care of yourself and the needs of your grief.

10. **You reach a point in your grief journey where you no longer believe you are going in the right direction and have no idea how to get back on track.** For a time, you may believe that things have really been clicking in your management of your grief journey. You are expressing your feelings. You are taking better care of yourself. You see the proverbial light at the end of the tunnel. Then you suffer a setback that leaves you dispirited and insecure about what to do or where to go. A counselor can help shine a light on what happened and guide you to discover new possibilities for continuing on your grief journey.

Even if you decide that your needs are not that acute, you may want to begin seeing a counselor just so you have *someone* to talk to. If you do choose to seek out a counselor, it is important to find someone who understands the grief journey. Track down the names of professionals in your community who may specialize in grief counseling or who have extensive experience in guiding those like you who have suffered a major loss. Interview any potential counselor and make sure that person's beliefs and attitudes about grief are in alignment with your own. This is an important partnership, one that can significantly propel you forward on your grief journey.

CHAPTER 3

Reaching Out

It helps to talk about it.

When you are grieving, you are likely to hear that advice frequently. The words may come from a spouse, a partner, a parent, a sibling, or even one of your adult children. You may be urged to talk about your loss by your best friend, your neighbor, your coworkers and colleagues, the people at your place of worship or those who know you at your bank, your grocery store, your doctor's or dentist's office, or your hair salon. You may hear this advice so often and with such insistence that it makes you cringe each time it is delivered.

"Talk about it? I don't even want to *think* about it!" you may want to shout in response.

When the loss is fresh and raw, regardless of how long it has been since it happened, and you are struggling with your own feelings, the idea of reaching out to talk to other people about your experience can seem threatening or intimidating. You may be convinced that talking to others cannot possibly help or may even make things worse. You may feel vulnerable and might hear your own counterarguments reverberating in your mind:

- "If I start talking about what happened, I'll just start crying uncontrollably and neither of us will know what to do."

- "They've got their own problems in life, so they don't *really* want to hear about mine."

- "If I share the truth about what I've been doing, thinking, and feeling, they'll think I'm crazy."

- "Once they learn about my real struggles, they'll just want to make the problems go away and give me all kinds of advice on how to 'fix' them."

- "Once I start opening up about my grief, I may want to go on for hours and hours, and no one has that kind of time."

- "They'll tell me that I shouldn't feel so bad because they know others who have it worse than I do."

- "They'll share details that I'd rather not know about other people's problems."

With so many concerns about opening up to other people about your experience, you can find yourself in a real conundrum. On the one hand, you may well recognize the truth in the advice that "it helps to talk about it." Underneath your insecurities about the idea of trusting in others, you may have a real and often powerful need to discuss what happened, to talk about your day-to-day experiences, or to share meaningful stories about the past before the loss struck. On the other hand, you may not know who to talk to and feel justifiably anxious about what to expect if and when you try.

Talking to a professional counselor can certainly help. An experienced grief counselor knows how to listen and can reassure you that your experience is normal, encourage the expression of your feelings, help you to accept the reality of your loss, check in to make sure you are taking proper care of yourself, and provide a context for what you may be going through. After considering your options, you may decide that you do not need a counselor right now and plan to seek the support you need from other people and other resources.

If that has been the case, you may be tired of avoiding other people, yet still feel the need to be guarded, so you stick to talking about superficial things like the weather, or even lie about how you are doing. It is possible to hide behind a wall of denial, insisting to everyone that everything is fine and that you do not need their help. However, the ideal is to see if that wall separating you from others can come down, if reaching out can open a door to trust, openness, connection, and be an invaluable aid in your healing and growth.

Can that happen? Can you really "talk about it" with other people safely and productively?

No one can say with any certainty how other people will react when you reach out to talk to them about your grief. It is one more unpredictable aspect of being on a grief journey. Just as each person suffering a loss responds differently to grief, anyone that you may bring into your circle of trust is apt to have a different reaction to you and your grief. Like you, they are just human and are doing the best they can. It is helpful to keep these two guiding principles in mind as you reach out to other people while grieving:

1. The process of reaching out to other people with the hope of finding support, understanding, and encouragement is completely worthwhile and a sign that you are taking charge of your grief journey.

2. You can greatly enhance your chances of cultivating truly supportive relationships and taking care of yourself emotionally by learning what may be reasonable to expect from others during this time.

Let's begin this exploration with the person that you may be closest to in your life: your spouse or partner. If the loss of your partner is the source of your grief, or if you are not in this kind of relationship, that closest person may be a parent, a sibling, or a very close friend. This person will likely be the one that you most *want* to talk to about what is really going on. You and this person have an established deep reservoir of love and caring. Your partner is a fixture in your life. That person has probably been there for you before, or vice versa, when one of you struggled with some other challenge or obstacle that life tossed your way. Furthermore, you are inevitably going to have regular contact with this person, so it would certainly help in many ways if the lines of communication and support were open and active during this important time of need.

It certainly *can* happen that way. If you and your significant other (or other loved one) have plenty of experience in listening to one another without judgment or needing to rush in and "fix" the other, that can pay enormous dividends now. Real empathy may be the most underrated and powerful relationship tool that exists. If you can rely on receiving empathy from your partner during the grief process, consider yourself truly blessed!

It is helpful to acknowledge that grief is a different kind of experience than almost any other life challenge. If this is the first time you have dealt with grief, it will likely take working together to come to terms about the many dynamics of grief. Try to keep in mind these few key points: there is no timetable for grief; physical symptoms are normal manifestations of grief; and the emotions that emerge from you are likely to be more intense and longer lasting than anything you have ever experienced before. If you do have a foundation of empathy and trust, along with a shared understanding of the grief process, then your prospects for receiving vital support from your partner or other loved one are certainly good. However, you should not be surprised if communicating about this topic is not as open and clear as you want or even expect it to be. Your spouse, unfortunately, may not be able to consistently provide the depth of emotional support, encouragement, and understanding that you hope to find. Why? Here are a few possible explanations that can shed light on the issues you might encounter with your spouse:

- **Your partner may be grieving, too.** This is obviously true after an event such as the death of a child. After suffering this type of excruciating loss, you both have had the world torn out from under you! Such an experience presents many complexities as you seek to share your grief while also recognizing that no matter how close you are, you each will grieve differently. There are many resources specifically designed to help couples cope with the loss of a child. However, your partner is also likely to be experiencing their own sense of grief if your loss involves one of your parents, siblings, or close friends, or if the loss comes via a health crisis such as breast cancer, or the loss of your job or business. One way or another, your beloved shares in your loss and will be affected by it, though the two of you may falsely assume that it is really just *your* loss. The fact that your significant other may be in the midst of their own grief can create some challenges for both of you as you interact about the topic. Talking openly about the situation can help you determine where your partner can and cannot help you.

- **Your partner's memories of past losses may be stirred up.** If your mother has died, your partner may recall their own mother's passing, even if it happened many years ago. Unresolved grief can be emotionally draining and disorienting, and it can cloud your partner's vision in seeing what is happening with you today. Again, talking about what is occurring can be helpful.

- **Your partner may be absolutely convinced they know what is best for you.** As you learn and practice new tools and strategies to cope with your grief, your partner is likely going to have a bird's-eye view of those experiments. Instead of merely being a witness as you find your own way of navigating this new terrain, your partner may be jumping in with answers for what you should and should not do. When those answers do not click with your experience, or if you simply disagree, friction may result. Then you will face the challenge of gently setting limits; for instance, you can discuss being open to receiving suggestions from your partner, but with the mutual understanding that it is important for you to make your own decisions about how you will manage your grief.

- **By helping with your grief process, your partner may reach a level of anxiety that they cannot easily tolerate.** The emotions and duration of grief can take anyone to new frontiers. Your partner is entering those new frontiers with you, and even if they strive to remain patient as you experience the varied depths of your grieving process, everyone has their limits. Your partner may simply reach a saturation point and make it clear that they are unable to listen or be fully present with you, at least for a time. That is normal, too.

- **Your partner may be too drained to offer continued emotional support.** If you are temporarily unable to carry out basic tasks and activities in your daily life, your partner no doubt is pitching in. Your partner may be doing more than their share of cooking and cleaning, errands, child care, etc. This is vital support, for which you no doubt will feel grateful and appreciative. Of course, you still may be looking to your partner to provide ongoing emotional support as well. The reality, though, is that your partner may not have enough reserves to fulfill that role, at least not on a regular basis. If that is the case, you may be better served to look to others for some or most of the emotional support that you need during this time.

The preceding list covers just some of the many challenges that may emerge when you turn to your spouse, partner, or other loved one for comfort and support during your grief process. If both parties are open and honest about their experiences at each step of the way, the obstacles can be dealt with successfully. You can find ways in which your spouse can support you and also resist trying to force a contribution beyond the other person's limits. Trial and error will help you both decide what is possible. Grappling with the complications of dealing with grief between two people who share such a close bond is bound to create some tension. Often just knowing and remembering that this person loves you and wants the best for you can help ease that tension and allow you to feel better about making some compromises.

If reaching out to your spouse or other primary loved one during grief can be challenging, does that mean that the prospects for obtaining support and encouragement are even less likely if you approach others who are close to you? Not necessarily. Again, having an awareness of what you might expect can be extremely helpful.

What You Might Gain by Reaching Out to Other People

- **A degree of caring and compassion that will simply help you feel less alone.** Some friends or family members may not have the right words or the ability to respond in the way you most desire, but you can often tell from their expression or manner that they really love you and feel for you. This in itself can help ease some of your painful feelings. If you choose to share with someone a part of your experience and they are at least able to provide a reassuring hug, take that in.

- **An ability and willingness to step in and assist you in practical ways.** If you tell a trusted friend or family member about your struggles with such tasks as sorting your mail, paying your bills, returning e-mails and phone calls, balancing your checkbook, or running simple errands around town, you may be surprised at how quickly they volunteer to help and how effectively they can manage some of these daily chores. Welcome this kind of support, even if the friend or family member is unable to be there with you emotionally. Their contribution may make it easier for you to focus on your deeper emotional needs.

- **A sense of humor that can offer a temporary antidote to your darker moods.** Most of us have at least one friend or family member who has a knack for making people laugh. When you are wrestling with deep sadness, anger, and even despair, you probably do not feel much like laughing. But if you allow yourself a brief visit with that person who has a sense of humor, you may be rewarded with a moment or two of laughter or smiling that helps to alleviate some of your stress. Occasional lighthearted interactions while you are grieving will remind you that life really can be seen from a different perspective, even if you cannot yet grasp it for more than a few moments.

- **Periods of listening with an open heart.** Not everyone can listen to the full expression of your grief experience or the many stories you yearn to tell without the need to step in and tell their own stories or even make judgments. But some of those who are close to you may have the ability to listen for a *period* of time with genuine compassion and an open heart. Pay attention to that response because it is their way of conveying the reassuring message, "I hear you. I'm here for you. I'm sorry you're hurting."

- **Invitations to get out of the house or just share a meal together.** You may be going through a period in which you really do not want to leave your house or apartment. And since you might not be eating much, you probably have no real desire to share a meal with anyone. Nevertheless, those invitations can serve as heart-warming reminders that someone is there waiting to escort you into the larger world, if and when you are ready.

- **Valuable tips for other resources for your grief journey.** Some friends or family members may recognize their own limitations in listening to you talk about your feelings and your grieving experiences. They may not even be comfortable being around you for very long when they can see just how much you are suffering. But perhaps they know someone else who has dealt with grief, or they remember hearing about a support group, a website, or a meditation technique that turns out to be right up your alley. Thank them for that tip and forgive their limitations.

- **Telling stories back to you about the loved one or life situation that you have lost.** If you trust in a friend or family member enough to share some of your fond and often poignant memories from the time before the loss, it may spark other memories held by that person. Listening to them share something they appreciated about your beloved may further enrich your own memories and what you seek to hold onto in the aftermath of your loss.

You have likely noticed a consistent theme in the guidelines related to what you might gain or expect when you reach out to others. It is the reality that you might receive different kinds of support, understanding, and assistance from different people. We all have our strengths and weaknesses, and when you are able to identify the strengths of those close to you, as it relates to their ability to aid in your grief process, you will discover what you may gain from reaching out to each person. The challenge is to also recognize and accept what each person is *not* able to provide. You will become more adept at doing so after spending time around those who care about you and allowing yourself to get close enough to them to determine how they will respond to you.

Now let's look at some of the important cautionary flags in your attempts to reach out to others.

What You May Not Want to Expect When Reaching Out to Other People

- **An ability to listen quietly to you for long periods without interjecting stories from their own life.** Face it, few people are trained to listen quietly and attentively, especially during these days of texting, tweeting, and Facebook postings that bounce back and forth faster than a Ping-Pong ball. It takes a great deal of patience and discipline to listen. If you expect that ability to emerge automatically in most of your family or friends, you are apt to be quickly disappointed. If you try talking about your experiences and the other person frequently cuts in to share something that you may think is trivial, you might politely say, "Someday, hopefully soon, I'll be able to really listen to you when you tell me about what's happening in your life. Right now, though, I really appreciate it when you're able to just listen." Their response will help you choose whether to share more with them.

- **An understanding of why you are acting so differently than what they are used to seeing in you.** Many people do not know much about the grief process and how dramatically it can affect someone. Whether you reach out to them in person or just on the phone, those who know you are likely to quickly notice your fatigue, sadness, or lack of focus. They may rush to their own conclusions, for example, assuming you are ill or overstressed. What they decide may not be consistent with what you are learning about the natural process of grieving. Even if they do not fully understand, do they show an ability to just "hang out" with you for a while and listen to where you are? If so, their company may still be helpful to you—within limits.

- **A degree of patience that allows them to accept that even when it has been a while since they last visited or spoke with you, you still have not necessarily gotten "better."** Many people have preconceived ideas about how long grief should last. Your friends and family care about you and want you to get well, so it is not surprising that they may become impatient waiting for that to happen. Also, they want to return to the comfort of being around the "real you." If this is what you notice when a friend or family member visits or contacts you, do your best to educate them about the grief journey. If they still show their impatience, they may not be someone you turn to for support during this time.

- **An acceptance of the reality that you are not looking for them to "fix" you.** For many people, being approached by someone in distress is automatically taken as a signal that the other person is looking for an immediate answer to their dilemma. Some people may react as if you have called them from a few miles away because you just got a flat tire and you wondered if they might be able to come and change it. "Sure," they say, "I'll be right there to help." So when you reach out to them now, they are still looking for the "flat tire" that they can fix. If they see that you are not eating, they bring you large plates of food. If they hear you obsess about your lost love, they change the subject to talk about someone you both know who is still very much alive. You may try to explain that you are not looking to be fixed, only to be accepted. Perhaps that will encourage a change in how they relate to you, perhaps not.

- **A recognition that even if you choose to back away from contact with that person for the duration of your grief, your friendship or closeness is not going to disappear forever.** This item points to a difficult challenge for many of those who are grieving. You may do your best to set boundaries so that you spend most of your time around those who are most able to support and understand you. At the same time, you limit your contact with those who may not be capable of meeting you where you need to be met, ideally doing so as graciously as possible. But that friend or family member may respond by calling you selfish or concluding that you do not love them or care about them anymore. You may lack the energy to relieve their anxiety, so the gulf between you may grow even wider. Sometimes, after doing your best to explain why you are responding as you are, you may simply have to wait until you are much further along in your grief journey to repair some suspended relationships.

Can Anyone Really Be There for Me?

It's back to the conundrum described earlier in this chapter. Whether it is your spouse, another family member, or a close friend, you want to reach out to others to share your grief. You need support, encouragement, and understanding from others. Yet you need to have reasonable expectations. And you need to be able and willing to set boundaries and limits in the name of taking care of yourself physically and emotionally. Yes, it is a lot to deal with. However, you know by now that the rewards can be great.

There is a very good chance that you will find at least one person or group of people who really *do* "get it." Who it will be may completely surprise you. Perhaps it is a clergy member or someone else from your place of worship, or it is a colleague or coworker. Maybe it is a relative who you had only a casual connection with before this happened. Maybe it is someone new who shows up in your life—quite possibly, from a support group for those in grief—who also understands what most is needed and appreciated at this time. Or maybe it is a friend who simply steps up to become the most trusted ally you could ever ask for. Whoever it happens to be, this is a person who not only can listen to you talk about your grief but also can provide unconditional acceptance of you and your experiences.

When you begin to see evidence that someone is emerging in your life who may be able to provide that extra degree of empathic listening and a willingness to be present with you in your grief, you can work to build a solid foundation for this supportive relationship.

Five Ways to Build Trust and Support with an Ally during Your Grief Journey

1. **Validate the friendship or connection that you already have with that person.** Thank them for any other time they have assisted you or simply been a good friend or relative. Mention what you admire in them as a person. Helping them feel truly appreciated will enable them to feel more comfortable being your trusted source of support now.

2. **Allow them to share their own previous experience with grief or with deep emotional needs.** Often, the best ally for someone who is grieving is a person who has been on that journey, or who has also experienced some kind of deep sadness, trauma, or tragedy. Not only do they understand the terrain, they also appreciate the rich benefits that can be gained from those who are truly supportive. They have a greater degree of insight or sensitivity that is allowing them to be there for you. You have a bond to share, which can help build trust and intimacy. So allow them the opportunity to fill you in on the background that is enabling them to help you. This other person will likely know when to let go of telling their own story and give you plenty of room to share yours.

3. **Be honest about your needs and what you are looking for.** You may even invite the other person to look over this book. The more they can tune into what you seek, the better able they will be to deliver it.

4. **Set limits on your times together, at least for a while.** You may be so excited to have found someone who really understands that you forget that they have a life of their own and do not have unlimited time to be with you. Setting limits will help you to pace yourself in reaching out to this person, just as you have learned to pace yourself in expressing your emotions in your safe space at home.

5. **Regard the story of your loss as a movie plot with a favorite actor or actress playing you as a character.** If you tell your story the way you would share the plot of a movie, you give yourself permission to go further with your sharing. It will help you get past any self-consciousness on your part as you begin to reveal your most personal details related to this time of grieving. This will allow your ally to better grasp the depth of your experiences and become at least one person who really knows what is happening to you, no matter what twists or turns your grief journey takes.

Reaching out to other people, like your grief journey itself, will be an ongoing process. As your journey through grief continues, you are likely to become more comfortable and more skilled at choosing when to trust others, and how to cultivate these important bonds. You may find that different people come in and out of your most trusted inner circle over time.

Do your best to show gratitude for anyone who has helped you on your journey. In addition, keep in mind that others may show up later to help escort you onto even higher ground as you make your way out of the abyss of grief and climb the personal mountain to your new life.

CHAPTER 4

Rebuilding Your Routine

The analogy of feeling as if your world has been pulled out from under you has been used in this book to describe the sensations that can occur after suffering a major loss. It is natural that your daily routine will be drastically shaken up as well. As discussed, you may find it difficult to eat regularly, sleep through the night, or to get up on time in the morning. Basic personal hygiene may seem unimportant, or, conversely, something to obsess about as a way to avoid facing your feelings. Resuming your work schedule or the responsibilities of taking care of your children and your home can seem overwhelming. The challenge of managing your finances looms as well, especially if your loss has taken the form of the death of a spouse or a parent, and created a whole new set of money concerns.

Your grief is likely taking its toll on your physical health as well. You may be losing weight and experiencing gastrointestinal distress. Or you are battling fatigue or suffering new aches and pains. You may be more prone to colds and other illnesses, or might just look pale most of the time.

If health-related or other personal issues had occurred before you entered into a period of grieving, you likely would have followed the needed steps to take care of yourself and regain your normal, healthy state. However, when grief has taken a hold, you may lack the energy or the inclination to pay proper attention to such needs. You may find yourself saying, "What does it matter?" The loss itself, and the sadness that has enveloped you, seems to have completely taken over your life. Nothing else appears worthy of your attention. And yet, as your loved ones and your doctor may be reminding you, taking care of yourself physically and becoming active again *does* matter. In fact, doing so is an essential part of managing your grief, just as much a part of healing as learning to embrace your feelings and reaching out to others for emotional support.

So how do you address these physical and practical needs?

The answer is: the same way you approach your other needs in the grief process. This means calling upon patience and flexibility, and remembering that your grief journey is unique and does not follow a straight line. In other words, there is no one definite way to start taking better care of yourself and begin to rebuild your routine; there is only the way that will be right for you. In this chapter, you will find tools and strategies to help you get a handle on this part of your grief process. These methods will point you in the right direction, but ultimately you will be creating a plan that best fits who you are and how you are responding to your loss. Use the ideas and tips that follow to begin reclaiming your healthy routine.

Five Tips to Help with Changed Sleep Habits

1. **Try to get up at the same time each morning.** You may find yourself going to bed much later than usual or waking up frequently during the night. This may lead to getting up later than you used to. That is okay, if you are able to accommodate the change into your schedule and responsibilities, but it may be helpful to get up about the same time each day so that you begin to reestablish a new routine. For example, if you used to wake up at 6 A.M., maybe you can now plan on getting up at 7:30 A.M. and begin your day with a few moments of meditation or deep breathing exercises.

2. **Schedule regular naps.** If you lost a lot of sleep during a restless night, a brief nap can help you maintain your energy and strength. Even if you do not sleep during the time you designate for a nap, just resting and closing your eyes can be helpful.

3. **Take a bath before going to bed.** For many people, this is a reliable way to reduce stress and prepare for sleep. While grieving, you are prone to absentmindedness and may forget about simple activities. Remember to consider this nightly bath as part of your grief routine.

4. **Listen to soothing music as part of your nighttime routine.** If you are suffering the loss of a loved one, the late hours of the night are not usually the best time to bring out the favorite songs you used to share with your beloved. Instead, choose relaxing music to help soothe your nerves and let you drift closer to sleep.

5. **Keep a journal and night light near your bed as tools to let you process feelings that may be keeping you awake.** When grief has triggered bouts of insomnia, it is easy to fall into a pattern of just lying awake in bed mulling over the same thoughts of hopelessness or despair. Doing so is not usually helpful in getting back to sleep. If you instead reach for your journal to write down what you are thinking and feeling, the act of expressing those disturbing thoughts and images may encourage them to recede, which may help relax your mind enough to sleep. You may note a useful insight or idea that you can reexamine in the light of day and consider how to put it to use in your grief process. Having a journal nearby provides the opportunity to write down the details of any dream that has awakened you from your sleep. Later, you may wish to reflect on any aspects of your dream that may be helpful, such as a clearer understanding of certain feelings or even a "message" that you can apply to your daily life.

Five Tips to Help with Changed Eating Habits

1. **Eat small, healthy snacks.** You may find that you are only able to eat one regular meal a day, or maybe not even that. While grieving, it usually does not help to try to force yourself to sit down at regular mealtimes and have some kind of breakfast, lunch, or dinner. Nevertheless, you need to preserve your strength. Small, healthy

snacks, such as fruit, yogurt, or nuts can help. You will know the healthy foods that your body likes best. You might consider protein shakes, energy bars, or supplements, but a consultation with your doctor may be helpful in sorting out the pros and cons of any meal substitutes. Natural foods are generally best for you, so try to eat these kinds of snacks at least a few times a day. Even a little at a time helps.

2. **Consider accepting an invitation from family or friends to go out to lunch or dinner.** For some people who are grieving, eating at home may be more difficult than eating out, especially if you have lost a loved one with whom you shared your home. A change of scenery may be enough to encourage you to at least try a cup of soup, nibble on a salad, or eat some bread and cheese. At the very least, having someone's company during the meal hour may take your mind off your suffering, at least for a while.

3. **Avoid unhealthy foods.** Staying away from alcohol and drugs is critical in maintaining basic health during grief, of course, but it is also important to refrain from junk food as your only source of nutrition for the day. Keep in mind that the urge for unhealthy foods while suffering a major loss is most likely a sign of emotional distress. See if you can practice safe ways of expressing your feelings instead of devouring candy bars.

4. **Drink plenty of water as well as healthy beverages, such as natural fruit juices and caffeine-free teas.** Dehydration becomes more of a threat when you are not eating regularly. Keep a bottle of water with you as you go around your house or at work. Juices and teas can provide further sustenance. Coffee with its caffeine, though temporarily comforting, will not help you manage your stress.

5. **Spend a little time preparing a favorite dish or meal, and then offer it to someone who cares about you.** First, this gesture can be an excellent way of showing your gratitude for family or friends who are assisting you with practical or emotional support during your grief. The payoff is that you *might* be tempted to sample some of what you have made yourself!

Five Tips to Help with Daily Tasks and Responsibilities

1. **Do not be afraid to ask for help.** Remember, the people who love you usually want to help. Many are reluctant to approach you, however, either because they are anxious about witnessing your emotional distress or they do not know *how* to help you. So, if you are having problems keeping up with basic household tasks or errands, call upon someone close to you to handle specific tasks. Not only will it help get things done, it may also open a door to greater closeness with the person you have entrusted with balancing your checkbook or walking your dog. You may want to ask a friend to serve as your designated contact person, someone with whom you can simply check in once a day to let them know that you are all right as well as get important messages or make sure that no emergency has arisen.

2. **Make checklists of the most important daily and weekly tasks that need attention.** Many things that you normally do as part of your daily routine just do not seem to be getting done while you are grieving, and in your current state you may struggle to even remember what those minor tasks are. It is helpful to make checklists to help focus on your everyday needs: sorting the mail, doing the laundry, starting and emptying the dishwasher, responding to e-mails, and so forth. For each item on the checklist, make notes about whether the task has been completed today, assigned to a helper, or postponed for a specific later time.

3. **Do not feel obligated to answer every e-mail or phone message.** Those who have suffered a recent loss are often overwhelmed by the number of expressions of caring and support that come pouring in every day, along with questions about their physical and emotional state. If that happens, trying to keep up with those messages can drain your energy and trigger surges of emotion that you are not prepared to cope with now. Give yourself permission to put on hold the act of responding to those contacts. It

may help to put a standing message on your voice mail or inbox that explains your situation and respectfully asks for the understanding of loved ones if you do not get back to them for a while. A friend who has stepped in to help with daily tasks could perhaps be enlisted to assist you in prioritizing messages and forwarding responses in your name.

4. **Be aware of particular tasks or activities that may trigger your grief.** Going through the belongings of a loved one who has passed away will take time as well as an understanding of the emotional impact on you. Do not rush yourself. For other kinds of losses, identify the tasks or situations that are the most likely to stir up feelings and decide when and how to best approach them.

5. **Be honest and clear about communicating your needs and your limits.** Be honest with yourself about what you are ready and able to handle at any particular period in your grief process. Then, tell others who are involved. If you have a job, talk to your supervisor or employer to fill them in as much as appropriate about your experience and negotiate any changes needed in your workload or schedule to help you stay on track with your grief process. Make clear to them that this is a priority! At home, talk to your spouse or other family members about what you honestly feel you can and cannot do in regard to your usual tasks and responsibilities. Emphasize that you need time to grieve. Help strategize with them about how to fill in the gaps.

The Need to Exercise

No matter how well you are doing with your eating, sleeping, and daily tasks and activities, it is critical to engage in at least some physical exercise. You of course know that exercise helps to reduce stress, and you have learned how the stress from a major loss can have significant effects physically and emotionally. Physical exercise can help keep your grief from advancing to a state of depression. Whether or not you previously followed any kind of exercise routine, it is important to get active now.

Of course, like many positive goals, this one may seem beyond your grasp at times when grief takes hold. You're tired, you're sad, you're not feeling positive about your life and your future. Exercise may seem like the last thing you would want to do. So how do you summon the energy and the will to exercise, even a little? It helps just to start somewhere and discover for yourself what will encourage you to follow up with more regular physical activity. Here are some ideas for starting points:

- **Take a short walk.** Even if you walk for as little as five minutes, near your home or office is helpful in getting your body loosened up, as well as breathing in some fresh air. If you do it once, see if you can commit to walking for five minutes twice a week. Try to progress to three times a week. Once you find a pace that you are comfortable with, stick with it for a while and try to make it a part of your regular routine. You can always expand on it, as you feel stronger and more engaged in life.

  If you struggle to walk for five minutes, start smaller. Is your mailbox located at the end of a long driveway or down one or more flights of stairs? Assign yourself the activity of walking to get the mail every day. Then try to move on from there.

- **Try dancing.** If you already enjoy dancing, this wonderful form of exercise may be a natural outlet during grief. Even if you have not done much dancing for years, or ever at all, you may find that it is something that fits in your adjusted daily routine now. You do not need to leave home to get started. Just put on some music that you sense will encourage you to start moving your body. Close your eyes if you wish. Do not be concerned with how you look, or how slow and awkward your movements may appear at first. You are not performing, and no one is watching. You are just trying to get your body loosened up. And you just may find that it frees up some of the pressure in your mind as well.

- **Go for a bike ride.** As with dancing, it does not matter whether or not biking was a part of your fitness routine before you suffered your loss. Just get out and try riding around your backyard or your driveway or a short distance down the road. If you successfully bike for a few minutes one day, try to repeat the activity the next day before inviting yourself to go a little further. As with walking, being outside will also help clear your head.

- **Do yoga.** If you have enjoyed attending yoga classes in the past, you may try to reclaim that outlet, staying for only as long as you feel comfortable. However, if you do not feel ready to be around others, or you are new to yoga, you can start with an instructional video or online workout program and practice at home. The stretching exercises will help alleviate stress.

- **Get out in nature and explore physical ways to express your feelings.** Just being in the woods or by a lake or stream can lessen some of your stress. You do not have to go far or map out a strenuous hike. Driving to a familiar and easily accessible nature spot is fine. Once you are there, see what your instincts tell you to do. You might walk around the scenic area for a few moments, for example. If you are feeling angry and frustrated, perhaps you will benefit from throwing rocks in the water or safely pounding a stick against a boulder. That is good exercise!

- **Visit a gym or fitness center.** If you already belong to a fitness center, you may have stopped going because you are feeling too self-conscious or you just do not have the energy. Perhaps now you can convince yourself to go back with the reassurance that you will not try to plunge right into any previous workout routine. Instead, try doing only a small portion of your usual regimen. Rather than going two or three times a week, start with once a week. See what your capability is and how it may expand over time. If you do not belong to a fitness center, see if you can set up a trial membership. Go at least a few times and experiment with different ways to engage your body again.

- **Do some gardening.** Whether you happen to be an avid gardener or have not spent time tending to plants or vegetables for years, consider beginning or reestablishing some kind of garden in your yard if you have one, or on your patio, terrace, or balcony. If it is not practical or beyond your scope to plant a garden of your own, ask a friend, neighbor, or family member who has a garden if you can help out there for a little while. If it has been a while since you have done any gardening, you may have forgotten how much exercise you get with all the bending, digging, lifting, and moving dirt around.

There are many other ways to get physically active, and with very little effort, you are likely to find what will work best for you. If you have young children or there are young children in your extended family or circle of friends, volunteer to visit with them for a little while. They will almost certainly get you moving again!

Fourteen-Day Activity Plan

This activity plan will help to guide you on your grief journey and the recovery process. As you rebuild your routine, you do not need to follow the plan exactly. Just use it as a guide or as an idea of daily plans to try out or add to what you already are doing. As you travel through your grief journey, some activities may become natural very quickly, while others may require a bit more time, effort, or help.

Day 1

Check in with your primary designated contact via phone or e-mail, just to let them know you are okay.

Day 2

Go for a ten-minute walk or engage in another physical activity.

Day 3

Spend fifteen minutes in your safe space to relax and take gentle inventory of your feelings.

Day 4

Take a few deep breaths and note any physical symptoms of grief that may be present. Make an appointment with your doctor if needed.

Day 5

Relax by reading a book or magazine for fifteen minutes.

Day 6

Sit for a few moments in quiet meditation or prayer.

Day 7

Review your list of daily tasks and responsibilities, and identify one area that may need your immediate attention or the assistance of a trusted helper.

Day 8

Open your grief journal (see page 52) and choose a new writing exercise to try or return to one that you previously completed and read it again, perhaps reflecting on what you wrote.

Day 9

Scan the Internet for a new grief recovery website to explore.

Day 10

Look over any recent invitations from family or friends to share a meal or just a brief visit and consider whether there is one that you are ready to accept.

Day 11

Try a new physical activity, such as biking, swimming, or yoga.

Day 12

Take a soothing bath before bedtime.

Day 13

Think about family or friends who have been assisting you recently and decide one way to express your gratitude.

Day 14

Spend fifteen minutes in a soothing place in nature.

Practice Makes Habits

As you explore some of these new tools and strategies to manage your stress, handle basic tasks, and get physically active again, you will gradually find yourself rebuilding previous routines or, more often, establishing new routines that you can successfully integrate into your changed state while grieving. Routines are helpful when you feel as if you have been cast adrift on the sea of loss. They provide an anchor, something to hold onto in what may seem for a while like endless days and nights. Routines help to restore structure into your life and encourage you to begin thinking about what is ahead rather than continuing to float haphazardly along. Taking steps to address your physical and practical needs gives you a way to balance all the times when your focus, intentionally or not, is much more on your emotional needs.

Yet even as you begin to expand your routines, it is important to maintain that balance. In other words, you want to be sure to include in your routine those opportunities to connect with your feelings or just relax without an agenda. As you have already learned, creating and regularly visiting a safe space where you can invite your feelings to emerge is critical to your healing. You may want to set aside time each day, or a few times a week, when you simply allow yourself to think about your beloved who is gone, or whatever your loss entails. Perhaps you will choose to use that time to reconnect with other memories. Or you may silently express your gratitude for having that person (or that job, or that part of your life) with you in the past.

Here is one more important reminder about adopting new routines in your daily life. You still can give yourself permission to reserve time for not doing *anything*. No activities. No plans. No exercise. In fact, if your instinct tells you that all you can do for an hour, an entire morning, or a whole day is to sit and stare at the wall, listen to that voice. Do not get caught in a "should" that makes you feel guilty for taking a break from all the new ways you have been exploring to nurture your healing. Sometimes going one whole day during which your only concrete action is to bring in the mail may be just what you need.

Grief takes time, and sometimes healing is taking place when you are simply sitting and being. With practice, and flexibility, you will know when it is time to move on to a new way of managing your grief and stepping a little more fully into your new world.

CHAPTER 5

Exploring New Terrain

As you have been learning, grief after a major loss can last a long time. The process is very different from healing a broken bone, with its fixed treatment and relatively predictable timetable to mend and regain your physical strength. When you are grieving, your heart is hurting, and it takes great care, patience, and understanding to reach a place of peace and summon the capacity to move fully forward in life again.

With grief, there is no simple surgical procedure to undergo, no cast to depend on to protect the bone while it heals. Instead, there is a vast supply of potential tools and resources to call upon as you construct your own pathway to healing and renewal. In a manner of speaking, you are the surgeon. You are assessing what you most need at any time during your grief process, and you are gently making the repairs. You are rebuilding the strength in your body, mind, and spirit. In that role, you can use all the help you can get!

The previous chapters have offered many useful ways to tend to your basic physical, emotional, and practical needs. This chapter presents new strategies and ideas that will help you gain greater strength and fortitude to venture further along in your grief journey. From starting a grief journal, to joining a support group, to trying meditation or guided imagery, the suggestions offered will add to the set of healing techniques you are learning about and considering as you continue through your grief process.

Five Benefits of Joining a Grief Support Group

In Chapter 2, the value and the potential of working with a grief counselor was discussed. Counseling can help you through the rough spots, help you see where you need to go next, and validate your ongoing experiences. Seeing a grief counselor offers the reliability of talking to a person trained in the grief process about your fears, your frustrations, your sadness, your confusion, or your anxiety about the future. Whether or not you have sought out a grief counselor, there can also be great value in seeking and finding a grief support group. Here are some benefits to consider as you explore whether a support group is right for you at this stage of your grief process.

1. **Knowing that you are not alone.** When you are suffering from a major loss, you may often feel as if you are all alone. Even if you have friends and loved ones around, you may feel that no one *really* understands what you are going through or can see things from your perspective. When you join a grief support group, you are instantly reminded that other people have lived through experiences similar to yours. They may even use some of the same language to describe their pain. It is a great relief to see that you are not alone after all.

2. **Telling your story to more people.** Telling your stories of grief to one person can be freeing and healing, but there is something about telling your story to a group of people that can feel even more empowering. You have more witnesses to your feelings, your beliefs, and your questions, and instead of looking at you as if you are crazy, they are nodding their heads in understanding and compassion. Your grief process somehow seems more real, more natural.

3. **Gaining insight from the experiences of others.** Anyone on a grief journey is constantly learning. When other group members tell their stories, sharing what each has come to see or understand, you are right there to soak up the lesson.

4. **Tapping a greater understanding by answering group members' questions.** When you share parts of your grief experience, it may spark the curiosity of others in the group. When they ask you questions in a respectful and supportive manner, guided by a skilled group facilitator, you may find yourself responding in a way that points to new directions you can take. You may encounter valuable "Aha!" moments that might never have emerged without a group member caring enough to ask the question.

5. **Providing a pool of potential friends and allies for your grief journey.** In a grief support group, everyone's presence is valuable. However, you might find yourself especially clicking with one particular person, and there may be mutual interest between you in extending support to one another outside the group. You will need to get clear on group guidelines, because some groups discourage individual members from getting together outside of group time. However, most grief support group facilitators actually encourage that kind of ongoing connection, especially after the group has ended.

Keeping a Grief Journal

Starting a journal during the upheaval of the early days of grieving can be very helpful as a means of expressing your thoughts, feelings, and experiences both before and after the loss. A journal offers a place for you to record what you may not be ready to share with anyone else, especially because you may not yet understand what you are going through, as your feelings are still so raw. Writing it down gives voice to whatever may be going on, and provides you with material to sift through and reflect upon when you are ready.

Your journal can become more than a temporary ally. As you go further on the grief path, you can continue to chronicle everything that is happening to you and write about new fears, concerns, and frustrations as they come along. You can enhance the benefits that your journal provides by giving yourself specific questions and prompts. Here are some ideas:

Ten Grief Journal Questions

1. What are your strongest feelings right now toward the person or situation that you have lost?

2. How do you define grief recovery, and what are the most important signs to you that you are on the right track?

3. Who has surprised you the most with their support on your grief journey, and what may be a good way to show gratitude?

4. What are you the most afraid of today?

5. What do you still feel guilty about, and how might that guilt be getting in the way of your further recovery?

6. What role, if any, does faith or spirituality play in your recovery?

7. What do you need to say to your beloved or to anyone involved in your loss?

8. What new strengths or abilities have you discovered in yourself during your grief journey so far?

9. What priorities have changed in your life since suffering this loss?

10. What is the biggest obstacle in your grief recovery right now, and what might help you overcome it?

Feel free to write your answers to any of these questions in brief or in great detail. You will know which questions are the most relevant and meaningful to you at any time, and you can always return later to a question that you skipped over.

Some journal users find that they gain more from an exercise if they begin with an open-ended phrase rather than a question. If this sounds like you, try filling in the blanks to some of these grief-related phrases on the next page:

Grief Journal Prompts

"When I try to think about the future, I find myself . . ."

"One new reality that this loss has led me to see is . . ."

"One memory of the time before this loss that I most want to hold on to is . . ."

"I will really know I'm getting better when I can . . ."

"The people in my life still have a difficult time understanding and accepting that I . . ."

Again, choose the prompts that seem to speak to you directly right now. Give yourself freedom to respond to them in any way you want, without concern for whether or not you are staying on the topic. Journal questions and prompts are simply a means to open the door to the thoughts and feelings you most need to express, explore, and understand.

You may want to experiment with the times that you will sit down to write in your journal. As mentioned in Chapter 2, it can be useful to keep your journal at your bedside so that if you are having a restless night, you can turn to your journal to express what is causing you anxiety. Your journal, however, is far more than a nighttime sleep remedy. You will benefit from journal explorations at any time of the day. You may want to set aside fifteen minutes every day, or at least a few times a week. Remember to create a safe space where you can focus on your journal free from other distractions in your life and without interruption from others.

As you become more comfortable with writing in your journal, you may find yourself coming up with questions and prompts of your own to address your current situation on your unique grief journey. It can help to bring in a photo or other tangible reminder of the person or situation that you lost. Looking at or touching that physical reminder from time to time while you are writing can stir up more feelings and insights. You can invite yourself to come more fully into the present moment by starting with a prompt such as:

"As I hold this photo of you in my hand right now, I find myself . . ."

Again, it's best to do these deeply personal exercises in a safe space, one where you can give yourself permission to break out a box of tissues. Don't be afraid to let go.

Writing a Letter to Your Beloved

Another option during your journaling is to sit down and write a letter to your lost loved one. If you have suffered the death of your spouse or partner, a child, a parent, or some other family member, take a few moments to tell that person what you are thinking and feeling about them. There is a good chance you have been doing that in your mind anyway, and maybe you have spoken some of those words aloud to your beloved from time to time. This is just an opportunity to make that experience more tangible and complete.

Fill your loved one in on everything going on in your life these days. Be honest about your feelings, not only the love you feel in your heart but any anger, guilt, or blame you are carrying as well. Tell them just how much you miss them, and just how difficult it has been to live without them. Talk about your hopes for the future. If it is a struggle to look to the future at all, ask them for their help.

Some people who are grieving find that writing to their beloved is natural. For others, it may seem awkward, especially at first. As with all of these new grief tools, consider it something you may want to experiment with once or twice. You will know whether it is something to pursue further. You also may discover that rather than write to your beloved, you can more easily speak to them. If that works for you, try not to let any self-conscious feelings slow you down. Talking to one's beloved, whether aloud or on paper, is a natural and healthy expression for many people who are grieving. There is nothing wrong with you for feeling inclined to connect with your lost love this way.

Other ways to maintain a sense of the loved one you are missing might include lighting a candle to represent that person, or putting up their name, as well as a photo if you would like, in a prominent place on your desk or somewhere else where you will see it often.

What if the loss that you are experiencing did not come in the form of the death of a loved one? You still can benefit from writing a letter to address whatever you are grieving for. If you have lost a part of your health, you may find yourself writing to the "you" that existed before the health crisis. If you lost your job or business, write to that entity as if it were a living being. Once you start, you will likely find it is not as strange as it may sound. If you experienced the end of a marriage, write to that marriage as if it were an actual person. Many of the feelings and expressions will likely sound similar to writing about a person who has passed away. Any loss that has triggered deep feelings and plunged you into grief is a loss that you can productively explore in your journal writing or in other forms of expression.

Journaling Tips

Journaling can be useful both when done in silence or with soft music in the background. However, it is best to keep your TV, computer, and phone all turned off. You do not want to divide your attention. You may find that your personal expressions change if you occasionally alter the location where you do your journal entries. Try going outside and sitting beneath a tree or beside a stream or any place where you feel comfortable.

Choosing the journal book that is right for you can assist you in getting the most from these exercises. Spend a little time looking for the color, shape, and texture that fits how you are feeling and what you hope to gain from spending time with this journal. You may want to consider using an assortment colored pens or markers when you write in your journal. Of course, in today's laptop lifestyle you may be tempted to do all your journaling on your computer. Who writes anything by hand anymore, right? Yes, it may feel different to sit down with pen and paper, but this form of expression tends to bring those who are grieving closer to their feelings than typing on a keyboard. It may be worthwhile to at least experiment for a time with writing by hand. You can always resort to a computer if you conclude that it is the only way you will get into the spirit of journaling.

Deciding if and when to share any of your journal entries with others is another way for you to take charge of your healing journey. You may choose to keep your journal entirely private. Or, if you are seeing a grief counselor, you might discuss with that person whether it would be helpful to share some of your journal notes during your counseling sessions. If you have found that one trusted grief ally who fully accepts you, perhaps you may want to read parts of your journal with that person as another way of letting them into your world. If you are married, and if the lines of communication with your spouse seem to be open enough, you might consider what to reveal from your journal within the framework of that relationship. But if you conclude that keeping your journal entirely to yourself is best for you, respect your own decision. Keep your grief journey in a safe and secure place, where no one is apt to come across it accidentally.

As you turn to your journal more regularly, do not forget that journaling is useful when you simply need to vent about the latest challenge or struggle. Think of your journal as another friend who is able to sit and listen to you without passing judgment.

Five Creative Approaches to Expressing Your Feelings

Writing and talking are not the only productive ways to explore the feelings and experiences associated with grief. Many people who are grieving successfully utilize other forms of creative expression. It does not matter whether or not you consider yourself at all "artistic" when seeking to tap the benefits of these creative outlets. Again, this is just another way for you to go further in the expression and exploration of your grief. You are not trying to make something to show to a teacher or present in public. What you create is just for you!

1. **Draw or paint your feelings about your lost loved one or to reflect your own experiences today.** This can be an especially effective way to access those emotions that go beyond words. Try to allow yourself to capture the image in the most natural form, regardless of whether it looks "right" or not. Then sit back and notice your feelings as you look at what you have created.

2. **Try using clay or some other medium to make a sculpture of your feelings or your general state while grieving.** It does not matter if you ever "finish" the sculpture, or whether it looks anything like what you expected or wanted it to be. Whatever you make will have meaning and value for you.

3. **Make a collage to represent the different feelings and experiences that capture your grief.** For some people, this manner of creative expression is a bit easier because it feels less like "doing art" and more like doing a project back in kindergarten. It does not matter if the supplies you choose are directly related to your loss or not. The creation itself will represent what you need to see.

4. **Create your own song or video as a tribute to your beloved or as another way to express your feelings while grieving.** Do not worry about how silly or corny it may look or sound. If you cannot seem to find the right words to write a song of your own, feel free to use song lyrics you already know to create a musical collage or make a CD mix that integrates several songs you like.

5. **Write a poem that brings to life some part of your grief journey.** Do not worry about whether or not it rhymes, and feel free to make your poem funny, angry, sad, or some combination of all three. After all, that is what the grief journey usually is: an imperfect blend of different feelings and emotional states.

Three Meditations for Your Grief Journey

Meditation is another practice that can assist you in managing your grief and exploring the new directions in which your grief may be taking you. You do not need any previous experience with meditation to begin doing it on your own. Meditation, like prayer or spending time in nature, is simply one more tool to help you relax and gently take inventory of your experiences as well as what you may be called to do next. With a little research, you will find many CDs that offer simple guided meditations as well as guided imagery, a technique that helps you focus and direct your imagination. Here are a few meditation techniques to help you get started.

1. **Working with your breath.** Find a comfortable position, either sitting or lying down. Close your eyes and try to relax. Breathe fully and easily, noticing each time as you inhale and exhale. After a while, bring in key words to reflect something you'd like to let go of more (exhale) and something you'd like to bring into your life more (inhale). For example, as you breathe in, you might think of the word "trust," and as you breathe out, you might think of the word "fear." For several moments or longer, maintain this focus of breathing in "trust" and breathing out "fear."

2. **Progressive relaxation.** For this meditation, it is usually advisable to lie down in a comfortable place. Begin by taking a few deep breaths from your belly. Then begin to imagine that you are relaxing each part of your body. Start down at your toes. Imagine that you are tensing your toes, and then invite the experience of relaxing your toes. Follow the same procedure as you move on to your feet, your calves, your thighs, your lower abdomen, and on up to your chest, arms, fingers, hands, throat, neck, face, and forehead. Then rest quietly for a few moments. This meditation may not only help to alleviate immediate stress, but also to ease your ongoing anxieties and concerns.

3. **Imagine a relaxing scene.** This is another meditation that can help you feel better in the moment while also reducing the grief-induced stress in your day-to-day life. You can repeat this meditation exercise any time that you would like to just slow the chatter in your mind or feel a bit more secure in your experiences. After getting comfortable and taking a few deep breaths, imagine yourself being in one of your favorite spots, somewhere soothing, relaxing, and pleasurable. It is fine to make up an image of such a place. It may be the ocean, the top of a snow-capped hiking trail, an open meadow, or a grove of trees along a stream. With just a little experimentation, you will know which scene

will work best for you. Once you have invited this scene into your mind, simply imagine yourself staying there for a while, just taking in the sights and resting. No need to do anything or figure anything out.

If guided meditations do not click for you, you may gain some of the same benefits simply by spending a few minutes each day practicing deep breathing, without adding words or imagery to the experience. You do not even have to get into a "meditative posture" to do it. Just put down anything you are holding onto and take a few deep breaths right where you are: at your desk, in the kitchen, on the sofa, in your bed, etc. After you feel complete, you can resume your activity. As you do this, you will likely notice you are letting go of some of your anxiety. Your deep breathing may even inspire a new insight or question that you will want to record in your journal.

Nature Is Still Calling

As already mentioned, simply being in nature can foster relaxation and peace during the tumultuous periods of grieving. You may discover that going back to your favorite nature spot can provide even more opportunities for discovery and healing as you move further along in your grief journey. Taking frequent walks or bike rides and blocking out time just to sit in nature is an excellent way to nurture your mental, physical, and emotional healing and growth.

Sometimes you may find that it is best to spend time in the woods, mountains, or near water with no specific plan or agenda. To rest and relax for a few moments is a valuable goal in itself. However, you may want to experiment with grief-related exercises while in nature. For example, if you find yourself at the ocean with a degree of privacy, try shouting the name of your beloved out toward the sea. Alternatively, pick up a stick or shell and sketch a picture in the sand that represents some part of your grief experience. If you are standing on a hillside, grab a stone and toss it over the edge (after checking to make sure no one is in harm's way, of course!), perhaps giving it a name related to something you would like to let go of. If you are in a forest, build a large pile of leaves and then toss them up in the air—this is another great way to release something you are holding onto.

Sometimes you do not even have to step far from your home to have an experience of being with the natural world. If you look outside and notice that it has begun to rain or snow, dress appropriately and take a brief walk in the elements. Feel the raindrops in your open palms or catch a snowflake on your tongue. Welcome any laughter or unexpected feeling that may come along.

Yet another way to invite progress on your grief journey is to visit inspiring places: a museum, a beautiful building, or a natural vista. Take your journal along in case you are moved to write if something important emerges, or just drink in the wonder before you. Perhaps you can encourage a similar response by doing something inspiring yourself, such as planting a tree or donating a few books to the library. While you are there, you can spend a few moments browsing through the shelves for inspirational reading. Rather than looking for another grief-related book, you may be drawn to read the autobiography of someone who overcame pain and hardship to make a significant contribution to the world.

Talking to God

For many people dealing with grief, God is an integral part of the process. For others, this may not be a realm for deep exploration. The experience of grief may open a door to a new understanding of God and religion. If your own beliefs include a personal relationship with God, or another supreme being or spiritual source, let's look at how your grief journey may be further shaped by this connection.

Sometimes the loss of a loved one, especially via a tragic accident or sudden illness, can shake the foundation of one's belief in God. Have you found yourself asking, "How could God allow this to happen?" If so, you are certainly not alone in questioning how, for example, a loving God could stand by and watch an innocent child die. This kind of expression may be only a brief manifestation of your overall feelings of anger and a sense of injustice—another way of saying, "This isn't fair!" It doesn't necessarily mean that you no longer believe in God. In fact, cursing or blaming God can be interpreted as confirmation that you really do believe there is some greater force and that life is not entirely random.

If these troubling questions and feelings about God persist, you may choose to discuss them with a clergy member, or perhaps a friend who shares your faith. However, if someone insists that what you are feeling is "wrong," remember that grief evokes all kinds of feelings and conclusions that are simply part of the process. As you continue on your grief journey, it is quite likely that the words you have to share with God will shift, and that God can once again become the incomparable presence and ally you have depended on in the past.

Knowing how to talk to God while grieving is something that will emerge from your own heart. Whether you communicate through specific prayers or your own informal words, you probably know better than anyone else does the expressions that will open this vital channel of love and inspiration. However, if you are seeking more options for directing your talks with God, here are some possibilities. You may already be noticing that your communication is reflecting many of these suggestions.

Five Possible Ways to Talk to God While Grieving

1. **Asking God for comfort and strength.** When your world has been knocked to pieces, asking God for help just to get through the storm is a natural inclination. So is reaching out to God during any new phase or experience in the grief process. Sometimes you may find yourself beginning your talk with this kind of admission: "Help me, God, I have never been through anything like this before." That's so true with grief!

2. **Asking God what to do or where to go next.** Feeling lost and directionless is a natural response to grieving. It can take a long time to navigate through the grief process and reach a new place. If you ask God for any kind of clue of what to expect, you may not receive a concrete answer. You may, however, receive an

important reassurance that God is present and will always be with you as you maneuver through the next difficult and frightening steps on your journey.

3. **Asking God all those "why" questions.** "Why did this happen?" "Why must life be so painful?" "Why is it taking so long to feel better?" Just giving voice to these kinds of questions, no matter how irrational or impossible to answer they may seem, can help lighten the burden you are carrying. Any response that you receive from God can add meaning and depth to your spiritual experience.

4. **Expressing gratitude for God's presence.** If you have felt God as a guiding and sustaining force during the roughest days of grieving, you may naturally want to express your appreciation and gratitude for that. For many who are grieving, it is enlightening to come to the recognition that God does not prevent suffering and loss but *does* help us persevere so that we are able to go on with our lives. The simple act of expressing gratitude can be liberating. If there is something to be grateful for, perhaps there can be something to live for as well.

5. **Thanking God for the opportunity to have loved.** You hurt while grieving over losing someone or something that you loved. Grief, in that regard, can be seen as the cost for having loved. And yet, even as you suffer, you may come to see as others have that you have no regrets for the depth of love that you felt while your beloved or your valued life situation was present. You were granted the opportunity to love, and you said "yes" to it. If you believe in spiritual forces in the world, you will naturally want to show your gratitude for having had that opportunity and experience.

There are limitless ways and forms for communicating with God about grief. For some people, God is an anchor to help them weather the storm. For others, God becomes a source of expanded awareness and understanding of the deepest realities of life. As you courageously march forward on your grief journey, pay attention to the role that God may play in helping you find your way.

CHAPTER 6

Facing the Future

Most grief experts agree that after suffering a significant loss, it is wise to put off major decisions in your life for a while, perhaps several months, a year, or even longer. Why is this important?

Remember that grief is a multidimensional experience: your heart has been wounded, your body systems have been knocked out of whack, and your mind has been clouded over. In the early days of grieving, you are reeling from what happened and most likely spending almost all your time and energy looking *backward* at the events surrounding the loss and your poignant memories from the past. You probably have little or no ability to focus on looking *ahead* at how to redirect your life in a clear, positive way.

If you do try to make major decisions too soon after a loss, it is very likely that your choices will be misguided and leave you with regrets or a steeper hill to climb. Selling your home and moving far away while still grieving, for example, can take away your primary sources of support and assistance. Your urge to move may arise from a natural emotional response to your situation, that is, it may be triggered by a vague notion that you can't go on where you are, so if you just leave maybe it will magically get better. It won't. Even if moving becomes more of a financial necessity after the loss of a spouse or a job, it is best to hang on for a while to give yourself a chance to start thinking more clearly. It will be easier to weigh your options and plan effectively when your anxiety has lessened somewhat.

If your husband or wife passed away, or your marriage ended due to divorce, it may be tempting to rush into a new intimate relationship at the first opportunity and dive right into a long-term commitment or a new marriage. Relationship counselors will tell you that is an almost surefire recipe for greater heartache. You need time to grieve over the death of the person or relationship and to discover who you are as a single person before you can thoughtfully begin to consider that kind of closeness and vulnerability with someone else. Similarly, if you recently lost a job or your business, the first weeks in the wake of the loss are not likely to be the best time to sort out your next prospects and map out a new plan. You do not want to be driven by sadness, desperation, or nostalgia when making those next job and career decisions. The grief that stems from losing a beloved pet similarly needs time before you can really open up to a new animal companion. You may be better served by declining any initial offers from friends to take on a new cat or dog right now.

This guidebook has invited you to explore how grief requires patience, understanding, and a willingness to embrace and examine your emotions. You now know that the grief process is a multifaceted journey during which your endurance and your faith will be tested again and again. The most effective approach is to be as fully present with your day-to-day, moment-to-moment experiences as you possibly can. Trying to look ahead too soon can detract from that effort.

When you are in the midst of grieving, you usually do not *want* to consider the future. Hopelessness may color every possibility, making it all just seem too scary and too gloomy. Gradually, however, your outlook will shift. You can come to recognize and accept that there *is* a future, and while it may not yet seem like a shining light is beckoning you forward, at least you know there is something else there, waiting for you to enter into it and navigate. Of course, decisions *do* need to be made—little by little and over time. As you work through your grief, you will see that you have a responsibility to yourself and to others who rely on you to face the future and to step back into a world that in some ways may seem the same while in other ways may appear entirely different.

After all, you are different, too. On your personal grief journey, you have been learning, growing, and healing. Your resilience and strength have been tapped, yielding inner changes that are likely to shape your outer choices and challenges going forward. You may not yet know exactly how it will all come together, but the rebuilding of your life has begun. Time might have seemed to stand still while you were initially dealing with your loss, but now you can again perceive and even welcome its forward-moving nature.

Ten Tips for Facing the Future after Grief

1. **Define your "new normal."** After managing grief for an extended time, you no doubt have noticed many changes in yourself. Your routines have been altered. Your perspective has shifted. Your emotions may have become more intense and more prevalent. You may be experiencing many other changes. Some of them may stick over the long haul, while others may fade away. It is helpful to assess this "new normal" state you are in and to describe it for yourself in a way that makes sense to you. Explain what is good about it, but acknowledge what you still do not like about it.

2. **Use positive self-talk to encourage your belief in the future and your capacity to embrace it.** During the most tumultuous period of grief, you probably heard yourself uttering all kinds of negative words and phrases reflecting the state you were in and your outlook on life. Now may be the time to experiment with embracing the other side. Try reassuring phrases like, "I move forward with clarity and strength of character," or "I now have the support and the resources to make important choices and decisions," or "I step into the future slowly and carefully."

3. **Take an inventory of your current values.** Knowing and naming your values is a helpful exercise at any juncture in life. Your values can be a powerful and positive force in shaping your choices and building the kind of life that is satisfying and rewarding for you. After surviving the maelstrom of grief, you may find that many of your core values have been reaffirmed and strengthened. At the same time, new values may have emerged. By thinking about and listing your values today, you will naturally be on stronger footing to face tomorrow.

4. **Rethink your priorities and set realistic goals.** It is not likely that you will have clear, large-scale goals for every aspect of your life as you slowly come through the other side of grief. By first identifying your real priorities, you will be better equipped to set smaller-scale, realistic goals that will reflect and affirm what is important to you in going forward.

5. **Consider the most important personality traits of the person or situation you have lost and brainstorm how you might embody those traits more in your life.** This can be an excellent way of honoring the memory of a loved one who has died, while also bringing important qualities and abilities into your life. If the loved one who is gone always impressed you with their calmness, for example, perhaps you can embody more of that calmness as you move further along on your grief journey. Or if the trait you identify is a sense of humor, think about ways in which you may invite humor into some of the choices you are considering.

6. **Protect your emotional vulnerability when you witness others close to you suffering a loss.** You may notice a yearning and a willingness to step in and help loved ones who have suffered a loss, noting how you have learned new skills and utilized new resources that you would like to share. The next chapter discusses ways in which you may choose to volunteer to assist others in life situations somehow related to your grief path. However, when your grief is still relatively fresh, and you see someone else suffering, it is also quite possible that your own feelings of grief and pain will rise to the surface. It is okay to pace yourself. You may need to back away briefly so that you do not backslide on your own journey.

7. **Make sure to continue to take good care of yourself physically.** After all the extra attention that you have been devoting to your physical state, it is easy to revert to bad habits as you turn your attention to the future. It is just as important that you eat right, sleep regularly, and get plenty of exercise after you have been feeling better for a while. With your doctor's guidance, you may decide to continue using vitamins, health supplements, pain relievers, or other new aids.

8. **Allow new people onto your primary support team.** During the worst of times of your grief journey, you may have relied heavily upon your grief counselor or a trusted ally who encouraged your emotional expression and accepted you as you were during the "crazy" times. People who have played those roles may remain

vital to you as you rub the dust from your eyes and survey the new landscape ahead. Now, however, you may want to seek and embrace new members of your support team. Family or friends who may not have been capable of supporting you emotionally may have excellent guidance or encouragement for decisions you are making now. You may find new friends emerging who have successfully managed major transitions in life and are eager and willing to share their wisdom with you.

9. **Consider using a daily compilation of inspirational sayings or meditations.** Many resource books offer daily sayings to help stay centered during times of change. Look for a book that is a good fit for you. It does not matter if it specifically relates to the grief journey or not. One of many grief-oriented resources is *Healing after Loss: Daily Meditations for Working Through Grief* written by Martha Whitmore Hickman. Here are two examples from that guide: "At the bottom of the well, one can look up and see the sky," and "I will step into the unknown dark, trusting I will be safe."

10. **Take special measures to prepare for holidays, birthdays, anniversaries, and other celebrations.** As you move through grief, much about your future may still remain unknown for quite some time. However, some aspects are far more definite. Specifically, you know you will encounter milestone events every year that may be potential triggers for your grief, while also offering you an opportunity to observe the occasion in a manner consistent with your new abilities and priorities.

Whether it is the arrival of milestone events, new jobs, new homes, new relationships, new financial outlooks, new habits or a return to old situations that will never feel quite the same—life is going forward. Step by step, moment by moment, you will be finding your place in it.

No matter what you do to help face the milestone and celebration days that will come often and regularly, it will help to be patient with yourself and recognize that setting limits is normal and healthy for those who are grieving. It is also natural that you may experience the kinds of mood swings and unpredictable behavior that you thought had passed months or years ago. Keep in mind that this too is simply part of the grief journey. The calendar will continue to usher in new birthdays, new holidays, and new anniversaries. You are going to find ways to deal with them.

Five Tips for Dealing with Holidays, Birthdays, and Other Celebrations

1. **Set realistic expectations.** If you assume that when a favorite holiday such as Thanksgiving comes you will enter into it with the same jovial spirit you have in the past, you are likely to be disappointed. Remember, grief affects almost every aspect of your life. This includes holidays and celebrations. Your grief-induced sadness may be intensified by seeing others who seem happy and carefree, and you will certainly miss your departed loved one. Since grief is unpredictable, you may not know exactly how those milestone days and celebratory events will turn out, but just knowing they will be different helps you absorb whatever the experience may be.

2. **Prepare for the event by walking through your anticipated experience.** Take a few moments to consider who is going to be there for the event, whether it is a family-oriented holiday, your birthday, your beloved's birthday, your wedding anniversary, or another milestone event. Think about how the occasion will be observed. Imagine you are already at that day and watch it unfold in your mind, step by step. Make a plan for what you may need to do to help you get through it: talk to your loved ones about your needs and concerns, limit the time you spend with others, and give yourself permission to take a brief walk. Remind yourself that you are not being selfish when you are taking care of yourself, regardless of what others may say or think.

3. **Proactively choose how you will spend the anniversary of your loss.** The anniversary date of the death of a loved one, or any major loss, is often an especially difficult challenge for those

in grief. Like it or not, the day is going to come. So is the period leading up to it, which often brings a new wave of sadness and despair with it. Rather than simply wait to see how bad the damage will be, it is healthier to shape the day in a personal manner. Brainstorm about how to nurture yourself while also finding ways to honor your beloved. Perhaps a visit to the spa is in order, or a picnic in the park. You may prefer a two-day getaway or a quiet dinner at home followed by a soothing bath. You may feel the desire to look at old photos, or you may choose to set them aside during this emotional period. Calling upon your trusted ally and supporter for companionship or a listening ear may help. Since these anniversaries will continue to have significance with each passing year, you will gain practice at choosing how to approach them.

4. **Make new holiday traditions.** When those who are grieving discover that it may be too painful or awkward to celebrate family holidays such as Thanksgiving with the same familiar traditions, they may decide to create an entirely new way to spend the day. If you find yourself in this situation, be proud—it takes real courage to go against the grain of long-established family traditions—but some loved ones may judge or criticize your need for your decisions. If this happens, simply communicate with them about why you need a change, remind them you still love them, and find alternative ways to share a connection before or after the holiday. Then make your own holiday, in your own style, honoring your grief journey and your emotional vulnerability. You may surprise yourself at how imaginative you can be in recreating a major holiday!

5. **Include your lost loved one in the celebration.** If you have lost a spouse or partner, a child, a parent, or a sibling, you know that this person will be there in your heart during the celebration. You may even find yourself blurting out an expression like, "You should be here!" It's natural to make that person's presence somehow real. Find a safe space and a few moments to talk privately to

your beloved. Choose some object or physical reminder of your lost loved one to carry with you or put in a prominent place. Give yourself permission to talk to others about your lost love—or not talk about them—on this vulnerable day that may be painful but is also an opportunity for healing.

CHAPTER 7

Remembering

Is grief ever completely resolved? Will you ever reach a point at which you can say, "It's over now"? Will you finally arrive at a place where the pain and sadness are gone and you never again encounter grief triggers that send you reeling back into the abyss? Will the yearning for and daily missing ever disappear for that person or that situation?

If you have been traveling along the grief path for a while, you are probably well aware that the short answer to questions like these is "no." And as you probably have come to understand, that answer does not paint the full picture. Not by any means. By following your grief journey with careful attention and a gentle spirit, you can certainly reach a place of peace and acceptance of your loss. It can rest in a mostly quiet place in your heart, and when it does stir again, you will have the means to hold it lovingly while it slowly subsides.

You can rebuild a life in which joy and laughter can occur freely; maybe not every day or every minute, but often enough to know that your life has become more balanced and complete. You will sleep better at night and awaken to what looks and feels more and more like a meaningful life, instead of just getting by. You will find that you can feel love again, even romantic love, if you choose. Experiencing romantic love may at times still be tempered by your loss, but it will be real and it will touch you. The capacity to feel love, romantic or otherwise, will sustain you as you face the future and enter new chapters in your life.

No, you may not find total resolution of your grief. You can, however, find a healthy reconciliation. You can grab hold of a life that generally feels fulfilling, even if it is not the life you once thought you would be living. Major change has swept through your life, and you have adjusted. Perhaps you have gained an awareness of how every ending is also a beginning, or that life always bringing changes, including painful loss.

Grief comes in layers. Something like the process of peeling an onion, as the layers unfold, a "new you" is gradually uncovered. You will likely discover that the experience of grief, and the depths of love that brought you there, have changed you forever. You have survived the storm, and quite possibly, you have even begun to find ways to thrive in a new manner. You may even say that you have had a positive transformation, coming away from this challenging experience with a stronger sense of yourself and your potential.

As you look back at the progress you have made on your grief journey, you may notice that instead of those days of constantly asking why this had to happen, you are actually experiencing a sense of gratitude for whom and what has helped you emerge intact. Your appreciation may be directed toward:

- Friends or family members who helped you pay bills, sort mail, clean house, or buy groceries when you were unable to perform those basic daily tasks.

- Your most trusted friend or ally, who showed up to hold you hand and listen for all those late-night distress phone calls or all those gloomy mornings.

- A grief counselor, doctor, or clergy member who helped you become attuned to your physical, emotional, and spiritual needs when that challenge seemed overwhelming.

- The poignant song, soothing meditation, or trusted journal entry that you knew you could turn to whenever painful emotions flared up.

- The safe space that you created for yourself to embrace your feelings or just find quiet solitude.

- The lost loved one or treasured life situation that enabled you to love so deeply and usher in such a profound grief journey, and the new possibilities for life that you are now sensing.

Love connects you to another person and to a deeper way of living. Surprisingly, so does grief. The experience of grieving connects you to other people and to new places within yourself. In this renewed spirit, you may notice a desire to help others who are in grief and who are suffering because of something they must endure. Following this inclination can be a life-affirming experience, validating your own learning and reminding you that you really do have much to give. You might find yourself assisting others as a friend, or you may choose to volunteer with some group or organization that helps those in distress. Perhaps you will gravitate toward a grief center, a hospice program, or a support system for those suffering the effects of long-term illnesses. Stepping into these kinds of volunteer roles may be new to you, but you will most likely find that you are extremely well suited to help because of the ways you have learned to manage grief.

Five Guidelines for Helping Those in Grief or Emotional Pain

1. **Listen to the grieving person with unconditional acceptance.** Remember not to judge their experience, whatever it may be. Try to accept their harsher feelings and negative expressions about other people or the world as a natural part of the grief process.

2. **Resist the urge to give them answers.** Just as you had to find your own way, it is important to accept that someone else's struggles and confusion are necessary components for finding their own way to grieve. If you avoid rushing in with answers born from your own experience, you will honor that person's unique journey and help them take charge of where it is going. You certainly can ask if they are open to hearing about a related experience from your journey, but when you do share about yourself, understand that you are simply offering something for their consideration. You do not know what is right for them.

3. **Be curious.** Do not be afraid to ask the other person gentle, respectful questions related to their experience as it begins to unfold before you. As they respond to your inquiries, they may

uncover new insights or awareness. At the same time, you also may learn something from what this other person has experienced or what they believe about it. Remember, the grief process never really ends. The learning goes on, for you and for them.

4. **Allow room for silence.** If you are new to the role of helping others in emotional pain, you may assume that you need to get them to keep talking, to go on expressing their feelings. Or you may feel that if they pause in their sharing, *you* need to fill the void by asking a question or offering an idea for consideration. In reality, you may be helping them by simply allowing a few moments of silence after they have revealed a difficult feeling or have begun to wrestle with a new layer of awareness. There can be great power in silence, especially when that other person knows you are offering them a strong, accepting presence in which to share it.

5. **Know when to steer someone who is grieving toward more professional help.** Because you know how to listen and are offering a safe space to explore feelings, the other person may suddenly begin to reveal information that you interpret as a warning sign of detrimental or even dangerous behavior. If they admit to excessive drinking or drug use, or seem to be considering potentially self-destructive acts, you will certainly want to do everything you can within your role to ensure that they will receive appropriate professional support and guidance.

Always Remember

Now you have learned how to manage the pain of grief. You have in essence unpeeled the layers of the onion and discovered more of who you are. You have begun to adjust to a world that feels somewhat new and changed, and you are finding new meaning and new connections along the way. You have accepted the reality of the loss.

As has been discussed, however, just because you know the loss is real does not mean that the love for or the connection with someone or something has disappeared. You will keep feeling that connection, and you will keep on missing your loved one or whatever you have lost.

That is natural, too. In fact, the grieving process actually serves you by allowing that person or what you lost to maintain a prominent place in your memory. If you had tried to deny the reality of your loss, you would have risked stifling that love and enduring connection and tarnished that memory. Instead, now you know the value of embracing real feelings related to your loss—the sadness, of course, but also the gratitude, and so much more.

You understand the value of keeping tangible reminders of your beloved around you, and you have witnessed the importance of including your lost love in celebrations and milestone events. You see clearly that it is natural to face times when you are sad, months or even years after suffering your loss, and that you need to make room for that sadness. You also have to make room to be happy.

Sometimes these feelings may seem to blend. If you lost a child, for example, and one day you bring a new child into the world, you may notice feelings of joy right alongside a sense of regret that your new family member cannot meet their sibling in the flesh. True happiness, though, may come in your ability to bring the memory of the child you have lost right into your family life today. That is one example of the kind of understanding and opportunity that emerges when you have been willing to learn what grief has to teach you. As you keep in mind the need to never forget what you have lost, so too should you never forget what you have learned and gained on your unique grief journey. You may find that those lessons and inspirations can take you to places you never dreamed possible!

Resources

Books

Attig, Thomas. *How We Grieve: Relearning the World*. New York, NY: Oxford University Press, 1996.

Bartocci, Barbara. *From Hurting to Happy: Transforming Your Life after Loss*. Notre Dame, IN: Sorin Books, 2002.

Brizendine, Judy. *Stunned by Grief: Remapping Your Life When Loss Changes Everything*. Lake Forest, CA: BennettKnepp Publishing, 2011.

Daniels, Psy.D, Linda. *Healing Journeys: How Trauma Survivors Learn to Live Again*. Far Hills, NJ: New Horizon Press, 2004.

Feinberg, Linda. *I'm Grieving as Fast as I Can*. Far Hills, NJ: New Horizons Press, 1994.

Hickman, Martha Whitmore. *Healing after Loss: Daily Meditations for Working through Grief*. New York, NY: Avon Books, 1994.

Noel, Brook. *I Wasn't Ready to Say Goodbye: Surviving, Coping and Healing after the Sudden Death of a Loved One*. Naperville, IL: Sourcebooks, Inc., 2008.

Van Praagh, James. *Healing Grief: Reclaiming Life after Any Loss*. New York, NY: New American Library/Penguin Putnam, 2001.

Websites

centerforloss.com

griefcounselor.org

griefhealingblog.com

griefshare.org

griefwatch.com

grieving.com

helpguide.org/mental/grief_loss.htm

thegrieftoolbox.com

navigatinggrief.com

recover-from-grief.com

Emergency Help

The process of grieving is unpredictable. One day you will feel fine, and the next you may feel overwhelmed. You might even feel so overwhelmed that you think of committing suicide.

Remember, there are no right or wrong feelings when you are grieving. It isn't terrible that you are having those thoughts. But it is important that you seek help immediately so you don't act on them. If you find that you are contemplating suicide, there are people who can help you quickly. It's a good idea to familiarize yourself with the various resources available to you, should you ever need them.

The National Suicide Prevention Lifeline is a 24-hour suicide prevention service that is available to anyone and provides immediate assistance. Call 1-800-273-TALK (8255).

Veterans and their families can find resources and help online at http://www.mentalhealth.va.gov/suicide_prevention/. If you are thinking of committing suicide, you can talk with qualified Department of Veterans' Affairs responders online at http://www.veteranscrisisline.net/ChatTermsOfService.aspx. You can also text 838255, or call 1-800-273-8255 and press 1 to talk to someone. These chats are confidential and available 7 days a week, 24 hours a day.

Another veterans' hotline for suicide prevention and help is 1-877-Vet2Vet (1-877-838-2838).

If your native language is Spanish, you can speak to responders in Spanish at 1-800-784-2432.

New mothers who are dealing with postpartum depression can speak with someone who understands at 1-800-773-6667.

Anonymous and confidential online chats with trained listeners are also available at:

- https://www.imalive.org/

- http://www.7cupsoftea.com/

- http://www.crisischat.org/

Always talk with someone when you need to.

Index

Notes

CPSIA information can be obtained
at www.ICGtesting.com
Printed in the USA
BVHW040305140423
662305BV00004B/11

9 781623 153557